STAY BALANCED!

by

Karen A. Stansbury

Lakeland Terrier Press, LLC

Lakeland Terrier Press, LLC
P.O. Box 181
Washington Depot, CT 06794

Cover cartoon by Dave May, Custom Cartoon Art
Cover design/layout by Deb Tremper, Six Penny Graphics
Logo design by Kelli Mincey, Cre8tive Mind Designs

Printed in the United States of America

Stay Balanced! is a work of fiction. Names, characters, places,
and incidents either are the product of the author's imagination,
or are used fictitiously. Any resemblance to actual persons,
living or dead, events or locales is entirely coincidental.

Misconduct. A transgression of some established and definite rule of action, a forbidden act, a dereliction from duty, unlawful behavior, willful in character, improper or wrong behavior; its synonyms are misdemeanor, misdeed, misbehavior, delinquency, impropriety, mismanagement, offense, but not negligence or carelessness. Term "misconduct" when applied to act of attorney, implies dishonest act or attempt to persuade court or jury by use of deceptive or reprehensible methods. See also **Wanton misconduct.**

Black's Law Dictionary

For

Karen Goldstein, RN, RMT
Who introduced me to Reiki, Aromatherapy,
Reconnective Healing, Quantum Healing, and
Guided Imagery

And

Lori Breiner, DC
Who introduced me to Whole-Body
Chiropractic and Kinesiology Testing

Contents

PART III VERDICT

Part I Discovery

1. The act or process of finding or learning something that was previously unknown.

2. Compulsory disclosure, at a party's request, of information that relates to the litigation.

Black's Law Dictionary

CHAPTER ONE

The Psychic

The night after the Thanksgiving dilemma I had a dream. My husband's kids insist that Nick and I should move from the house to the garage. The resulting free space, they determine, will be adequate for their living requirements. Nick appears to be perfectly content with this arrangement. I awoke with trepidation.

That was more than a year ago. I should have listened to that psychic. Had I believed then that I was about to be propelled into the guacamole, I would have taken proper precautions. I would never be caught on a cruise ship without a wetsuit and shark repellent.

It began with a phone call. These things always happened during dinner.

"DAD, OH MY GOD, I'M IN JAIL!"

"This is Emma, Doug," I said in my soothing-the-distraught-divorce-client voice.

"LET ME TALK TO DAD!"

I watched Nick listen to Doug, his face a model of passivity. Here was yet another reason why I never reproduced.

"Is the young woman dead, or merely unconscious?"

Not good. I began to mix martinis for both of us.

"I'll be up there as soon as I can. Don't say anything more to the police." Nick took one swallow of his drink and handed it back to me. "Horseplay in the dormitory, apparently. One girl is in intensive care."

"What were they doing?"

"Playing hockey in the passageway. I've got to get going, Em. Can you call my sister and cancel Thanksgiving?"

"What about your daughter?"

"Oh, and can you call Deborah?"

Children should be hatched from test tubes and distributed at random. Moreover, holidays with one's family should be outlawed. Why would anyone encourage the company of the same people at seasonal celebrations that one had successfully avoided the rest of the year?

Deborah, at the age of twenty, was an expert on everything.

"No problem. We will be having dinner with Mom this year." Her voice was ever composed, ever controlled.

"If Doug is out of trouble by then."

"Dad will take care of the problem. Then Doug will be reminded that he is a disappointment to his family. Again."

"What do you expect? The guy is training to teach our nation's youth. Should he be bashing them in the head with hockey pucks?"

"If Dad had taken more trouble with Doug, this wouldn't have happened."

"Excuse me?"

"Doug has always felt neglected by Dad, and I have to protect him."

I sighed with boredom. For over ten years I had heard this soliloquy. "Why?"

"What do you mean, why?"

"Why are you fighting for him?" I moved on to the underlying issue. "Do you have any idea how difficult it is for me to coordinate what will make your dad happy with what I would like to do—every damn holiday?"

"You've always been…."

"This season is ghastly enough as it is."

"I know it's…."

"Just once, I'd like to get through this period of joyful festivity without some emotional outbreak regarding poor, slighted Doug. Do you think you could possibly pull this off for a change?"

I'd been practicing civil litigation for fifteen years. Who did she think would win this one?

Deborah burst into tears.

Nick was back the next morning. "I got him released. I hope the judge will buy the fact that this was an accident. What the university's response will be is entirely another matter."

We had a relaxed Thanksgiving Day brunch at noon. We brought the requisite treats home for the terriers, and sat by the library fire with our books until dinnertime. By eight o'clock, I had begun to dread Christmas.

On or about the first of December of every year, I wondered what on earth had possessed me to apply to law school. Litigation was not a glamorous profession. "Going to court" sounded impressive to the uninitiated, but to those of us who knew better, it was a curious dance that involved much wasted time and paperwork, and perhaps more importantly, a constant fear that if one got up from one's seat to make a dash for the ladies' room, one's case would be called and passed for several more hours. Factor into the equation the annoyed client who must pay the billable hours on the aforementioned, and the other annoyed clients who called the office to hear that one had "gone to court." Last Christmas season was no exception to the established pattern.

At nine o'clock Annie slapped a file on my desk.

"Ed needs you to go to court on this."

The Fischer divorce. Agony. I knocked on his office door and was summoned into the presence.

"They're fighting over visitation for the holidays. He wants to go to Aspen; she wants to stay with her family in D.C. Hearing's scheduled for ten o'clock, along with about five other matters. Try to work it out."

"I've got a riding lesson at four...."

"You know I normally don't dump my files on other people." A lie. "But I have a serious conflict." Can't be golf in early December. "I have to finish my basketball coaching resume by lunch."

Ed had four sons upon whom he has inflicted said sport. Not one of them was taller than five-six.

The Fischers lived in Westport and had filed for a dissolution of marriage in May. Bridgeport was relatively safe during business hours, when all the drug dealers were still in bed. I conducted my usual fifteen minute reconnoiter to secure a parking space, smiled graciously at the marshals who operated the metal detector, and waited the standard ten minutes for an elevator to the sixth floor.

McCook, Noles and McCook represented Leila Fischer who was forty-five at the time, and in dubious mental health. Although everyone in our office commiserated with Mr. Fischer, it wouldn't be prudent to say so, especially in light of the considerable retainer we received from her parents. She was waiting for me in the courtroom.

"We have to squash that worm, Em. You can't let him get away with this."

I approached the clerk—a short, balding specimen. "Emma Carbury on *Fischer*. Which judge is assigned to this case?"

"Calabrese. He had three cups of espresso this morning."

"Any idea where we are in the line-up?"

"Fourth. And the three ahead of you are temporary custody

motions." Egads. "Go ahead to Family Relations. I'll tell the judge where you are."

I herded my client out the door and onto a bench in the corridor. Her spouse and counsel were just emerging from the elevator. I felt her tense as if to spring and grabbed her arm just in time.

"We need to talk, Chuck," I said. "We're the fourth matter on the calendar and probably won't be reached until breakfast. How about a compromise?" I heard Leila mutter something anatomically incorrect, but chose to ignore her. "Would you consider Christmas in D.C. and New Year's in Colorado?"

"That sounds reasonable. I'll speak to my client." It was always refreshing to work with opposing attorneys who had brains. Most family lawyers wouldn't know the Practice Book if it bit them on the ass. Their one concern was racking up the billable hours for as many clients as possible. I turned to Leila who was grinding one inch red pincers into her palms. "If he agrees to this, we can be out of the building in less than an hour."

"Fine. But he doesn't get them until the 28th." That's the spirit. "And he pays the air fare."

Having duly reported our proposal to the judge, it was so ordered, and I returned to my Fairfield base in triumph.

"Ed's at lunch with Mr. McCook and a client," reported Annie. "He left you these." She indicated a stack of depositions from the Trudeau accident. Mr. Trudeau was struck from behind on the Merritt Parkway by a Greenwich housewife in a Range Rover, who had "just turned to talk to the children for a second." Happily, she had enlightened the officer who responded with this statement. "He is deposing their expert tomorrow at nine. Or rather, you are."

"It will take me all night to review these! Why didn't he let me know last week?"

"Bar Association dinner tonight. Matrimonial section. He forgot that he's the speaker."

I hoisted my supply of transcripts into the house later that evening. My husband was in his lair with a decanter of single malt, our Welsh Terrier, Macduff, and several volumes of the Connecticut Reports.

"How was Joy?" Joy was my Irish Sport Horse mare. She was smart, and a very talented jumper, and she knew it.

"Fresh. Where's Abby?"

"She shredded the comforter in the big guest room, so I put her in her crate."

Abby was our Lakeland Terrier. She was smart, had very sharp teeth, and she knew it.

"Did you eat?" I asked, kissing the top of his head. "Do you feel like spending some quality time together?'

"Can't," he replied, standing up quickly. "We're playing The Old Pucks tonight. Oh, and Em, your mother called."

My study was on the second floor of the house, so I could at once stare out the window at my perennials and avoid the refrigerator.

"Mom?"

"Hello, dear. I was wondering if you've spoken to your sister recently?"

"Wouldn't it be easier to call and speak to her yourself?"

"Don't be ridiculous, dear. I would never interfere in Kate's life."

"To which aspect of her life are we referring?"

"She was just promoted again, dear. But she wants to have another baby. Tom prefers to wait. I'm sure he has his reasons."

"Meaning what, Mom?"

"You know that I've always felt that Tom is too happy to rely on your sister's income. However, dear, about the holidays. Which do you want this year—Eve or Day?"

"Kate and I agreed last month that I would do Eve, thereby providing me with backup while Nick's kids are here. Then we'll spend

Christmas Day at Kate's, and Nick and I leave for New Hampshire on the twenty-sixth. Why?"

"I thought, if it's convenient for you, dear, of course, that I could take the train from Ridgefield to Warwick on Eve morning. You would pick me up and I could stay the night and go with you to New Canaan on Christmas Day. Kate could run me back in the evening."

Audrey was perfectly capable of driving ten miles.

"Fine, Mother. If Kate agrees."

"Naturally, she'll agree. I should hope that you both are happy to do whatever you can for me, especially in my situation. Wonderful talking to you, dear."

That night, I dreamed that my sister Kate and I are in the back seat of my red Audi, and Audrey is driving. We are hurtling forward in a zigzag movement, and suddenly we go over a cliff. We both shriek and brace ourselves, but the car stops abruptly at the bottom, and we get out, both unharmed. I am wearing a turtleneck sweater that is too tight. As we climb back up the hill, I pull the sweater off and throw it on the ground.

Then, I'm on a boat, traveling very fast along a canal. The water is choppy, but I feel exhilarated by the speed and the wind in my face. Both sides of the canal are decorated with colorful tiles.

I considered the gift certificate that Kate had given me—one hour with a psychic in Stamford.

"What am I supposed to do with this?" I asked, skeptical.

"You're supposed to sit there and let her talk," my sister replied. "The less you say, the better, remember."

"Why?"

"The bad ones get answers from you and play them back like they're readings. But this woman is supposed to be good."

"Yes, but why should I be sitting with her in the first place?

Kate frowned. "Because I'm worried about you. Your personality has always been volatile, and it's getting worse. You're drinking too much, you're yelling too much, and you're becoming a first class bitch."

"Thanks."

"You know it's true. You zip around like a crazy person with too many irons in the fire. Your practice, your painting, your horse. Playing hostess to Nick's gang in New Hampshire. I'm terrified that you're going to crash and burn."

"This is nonsense Kate. You know how strong I am."

"Yes. And when tough people fall, they really do." She pulled my hair. "I *don't* want you to end up like Dad. And you won't go to a shrink. Give it a shot."

I gave up. "What will it feel like?"

"Who knows? I'm sure that flickering candles will be involved. Just go with it."

So, I went with it. I met Ingela Johansson at her home the next evening. She was a healthy looking Nordic gal, beautiful, clear skin and ash blond hair pulled back in a bun. She spoke with a slight Swedish accent.

She motioned me to a small table. There was a chair on each side, and a row of lit candles in the middle. Also a box of tissues.

"Don't cross your legs," Ingela directed, and closed her eyes.

"You're a complicated lady," she announced. "Part of you is deeply rooted in your present life, but the other half of you wants to fly."

Remembering Kate's advice, I kept silent.

"You like adventure. But you don't like change. I'm getting art, color. You're very creative. You like to make things beautiful. I see fancy writing. Decorating. Do you paint?"

"Yes."

"You're intellectual; very good at your job, but it isn't fun for you. I see lots of papers. You work with people who eat nails for breakfast, but you're not comfortable with that. You want a change."

"Do I?"

"Yes. It will come. Be patient. That's your problem. You do everything too fast, and it exhausts you."

I wasn't going to let that one go. "I want what I want."

"But you can't hurry the Universe. Stop micro managing your life. You're putting one foot in front of the other. Learn to skate. You'll be happier." Ingela paused. "And give in to your emotions more. You don't need to be so practical all the time."

"I don't like being emotional, and I'm bored by drama. I can't problem solve when I'm upset."

"You'll make yourself sick. Do what I tell you."

It's difficult to glare at a woman when her eyes are closed.

"I see a house on the water, but it's dark. You should always be near water. Or on it, or in it. Water is healing for you."

"Yes."

"Nature. Large animals. Being in the country. This is important."

"I know."

"You're very close to your sister. You're going to get closer. Your mother—she's a problem. She was never there for you. She didn't protect you."

"No."

"Your father—he's all around you."

What the hell does that mean?

"You feel a lacking; a hole. He never acknowledged your achievements. You have a great deal of anger. Did he drink?"

"It was horrible. He ruined everything while we were growing up."

"The men in his family have been alcoholics for generations. The abuse was passed from father to son."

"But I'm a woman."

"He put all his attention into another woman in the family. She was always in the way. Your mother, or your sister?"

"Either one."

"This woman was a teacher."

"My mother tried to teach."

"Your mother, then. You got only criticism and abuse. And too much responsibility. I see a child who is really an adult. Your past has held you back. Let it go."

I didn't respond.

"Your brain is your fortune. Use it. You are going to prosper. You're going to have your own office."

"Maybe some day."

"You need the outdoors. You need physical activity. You aren't good in crowds. Avoid them. You're in a mid-life crisis right now. For another year. Everything will change. Don't worry so much. Worry saps energy. Trust more."

"That's very difficult for me."

"Trust the Universe. You're very powerful, very spiritually evolved, but your impatience gets in the way. Slow down. Be still. Do meditation and yoga. This year will be difficult, but then you will soar. Your totem is the hawk."

"Totem?"

"And you're going to cut your hair."

"No, I won't. I like my hair."

"You're going to cut it." She scrunched up her forehead. "There's someone who you can't trust. You think you can, but you can't."

Oh shit. "Who?"

"Deception and betrayal. Blind-sided. But you're very strong. You always go with your heart." She opened her eyes. "Heal your past. Deal with your present. And don't let anyone hold you down. That's all they want you to know now."

They? "But I need more information!"

Ingela smiled. "You see? Always pushing. Remember that there is no such thing as human. We are all powerful spirits, here to learn. Just let it go, and the answers will come."

Kate called the next morning, demanding a report.

"Well, she certainly had our parents down cold," Kate said. "Did you know about Dad's family?"

"If it's true. I've never bought into this other world, new-age stuff."

"Neither have I, but I'd keep an open mind if I were you. It sounds as if Ingela was dead-on about too much. Who is this person that you can't trust?"

"One of the partners? No clue."

"Well, watch your back."

"I believe in facts, Katherine. Not woo-woo nonsense from some broad who burns incense and has statues of angels all over her living room. I've been doing research on the Web. Even the most famous psychics, the ones who work with the Feds, only have about a ninety percent accuracy rate. Anything to do with the future is just a toss-up. Too many people with free will in the mix to make realistic predictions."

"OK. But I'm going to ask Audrey about Dad's family history, just to be safe."

I met Laura in Westport for lunch the following week. There was something so soothing about an enormous cobb salad and a sensible friend.

"Every few months a new crisis develops at my barn. Yesterday, while I was tacking up Ripple, I overheard Madeline tell one of the mothers that she was buying the business from the owners and firing Louis. Now what do I do? Stay where I am, or follow my instructor to hopefully greener pastures? I get plenty of political intrigue at the office. I ride my horse to relax." She buttered her roll. "Anything new at your barn?"

"Unfortunately. I've been taking two, one-hour private lessons a week for almost a year. Rich and Wendy have decided that they want to generate more income during the off-peak hours, and are leasing the grounds and some of the horses to the UConn Fairfield team during the day. This obliterates time and space for my lessons, and those of many other boarders, as well."

"So much for keeping the good customers happy! Are you going to change barns?"

"Not right away. I like the staff and I like Jeannie. The care is excellent. The owners are a nightmare, but are rarely visible. It's the total reverse of what we saw in Redding." Laura and I had met at a show stable where it was more important to have a tack trunk in the barn colors, and the latest custom jacket, than it was to manage the farm properly.

Laura sighed. "I've pretty much decided to go with Louis to his new barn. He's a good guy, and he really cares about the animals."

"How unusual in the horse show world."

My watercolor painting class met on Tuesday nights. Our teacher was a local artist who believed in instructing on technique and leaving interpretation to the student.

Pam was demonstrating a winter sky that night. There was the usual amount of unrelated chatter while she worked.

"Remember, variation is paramount; in your composition and in the colors you apply...."

"My daughter Franny is going to have more knee surgery done next month...."

"I saw the most amazing bird in my feeder yesterday morning...."

"We have to leave early for our granddaughter's birthday dinner tonight...."

"As I've said many times—the key to a successful landscape is a dramatic sky...."

"Emma, you're a lawyer."

Oh, Lord.

"Yes?" My Payne's gray had begun to run into my yellow ochre.

"My wife had an accident in Westport on Saturday."

"Is she all right?"

"She broke a couple of ribs and is wearing a neck brace. She's still treating." The phrase that personal injury lawyers love to hear.

"What happened?" I dropped some neutral tint onto my distant hills.

"Someone cut her off on the Post Road, so she skidded in the snow and crashed into a gas pump island."

"Any witnesses?" I tilted my three hundred pound paper to achieve the desired ominous effect.

"Our neighbor was in the passenger seat; she saw the license plate of the other car."

"Tell your wife to call my senior partner this week." I produced my card and wrote Gerald McCook on the back. I then proceeded to remove the block-out from my birch trees.

"Be sure to rinse your brushes between washes, or your colors will turn to mud...."

"Pamela, when you have a moment," Veronica whined. Every classroom in the world had a Veronica. Pam smothered a eye roll and strolled over to her table.

"When you apply a wash of gray to the shadow side of the tree, it will appear to be round and not glued onto the paper...."

I took a makeup lesson the following afternoon. Jeannie set up a gymnastic. This was a series of jumps that could be placed as closely together as the width of a stride, so that the horse appeared to bounce over one to the next. She announced that we would start with two—a cross rail and a vertical.

"Shouldn't I do a few singles to warm up first?"

"You know that Joy can walk to a four foot fence. She'll be fine."

I trotted Joy around the ring once and then zeroed in on the cross rail, remembering the basic rules that have been shouted at me often enough: eyes up, heels down, and wait till the base. We sailed over the first fence as planned, but a glitch developed before the second. Joy took it upon herself to veer sharply to the right, while I continued in a forward trajectory. Something very hard made contact with my southern-most region, and I found myself sitting astride one of the heavy jump poles. I was still holding the reins. Joy began to munch on the top of my velvet hat.

"Can you get up?" I noticed Ellie, the barn manager, heading toward us at a collected canter.

"I think so."

"Just sit for a minute. Is it your back?"

"No, it's my butt." What an attractive bruise this would be. "You're going to make me get back on her, aren't you?" I asked Jeannie.

"Absolutely. She can't be allowed to think this is acceptable behavior."

My most pressing concern.

"What spooked her?"

"One of the grooms came down the hill with a wheelbarrow. Something she sees forty times a day."

I managed to stay in the saddle for round two. I jammed every ounce of my weight into my heels, and we conquered the gymnastic. When Jeannie added another jump, I urged Joy through too quickly for her to notice any distraction short of a cattle stampede.

"Good," Jeannie said. "But you've still got too much of a death grip on the reins. Try more give and take with the motion of her head, especially over jumps. She's so powerful, you don't want her standing up because you're on her mouth too much. By shifting your weight in the saddle, and using your voice, you'll be working with her more, muscling her less. Joy weighs twelve hundred pounds, so she's always going to win in a battle. Remember honey, not vinegar."

There was still the issue of the rapidly growing contusion on my posterior.

CHAPTER TWO

Christmas Eve

I was not merely repulsed by the materialism of the holidays; I was also disgusted by the waste. December was a month of excess and fatigue, punctuated by endless obligatory parties and thousands of trees that were cut down for three weeks of celebrating, to be thrown in the compost pile in January. How many women felt as I did, and would they ever admit it publicly?

Wednesday night there was a message from Doug: *"Hi Dad and Emma. I'm up in Boston with Sara. I know we're supposed to go to your house on Christmas Eve, but Sara wants me to spend it here with her family. Would it be all right if I came over on the twenty-fifth, instead? I'm bringing Sara and staying at Mom's, so that would be easier for me. Love you. Bye!"*

"Don't say it." Nick prepared for battle.

"What? That your son is the most self-centered, childish annoyance on the planet? That his girlfriend *du jour* is more important than inconveniencing his entire family? That he tells us he wants a good relationship with us regularly, but then socks us in the teeth every holiday? AM I GETTING WARM?" Yes, the spirit was definitely moving me.

"He's better, Em. At least this time, he's given us two weeks notice."

"Oh, for God's sake! What *is* it with you people? No matter what that kid does, you make excuses for him. Christmas has been planned since before Thanksgiving and Doug knows it. There will be no alterations in the schedule. He comes Eve or he doesn't come at all. Unless you'd like to do the cooking, the decorating, and the wrapping this year?"

"I'll call him back," Nick said.

Thursday afternoon was my office Christmas party. We had agreed by vote that year to eliminate the gift giving, but the party was still considered mandatory. Ed, who was the managing partner, got up on the library steps to say a few words.

"I'm sure I speak for every partner when I express my appreciation to all of you for the work you've done this year. It has been an especially profitable one. We have been able to make many—and I'm sure you will agree—necessary changes, such as the new wing and the updated computer system. We were also able to hire several new associates. Most important to me, however, is the addition of my son Mark to our legal staff. As you know, Mark passed the bar and was sworn in last week." He raised his glass. "Welcome, Mark!"

The staff: "Welcome, Mark!" No mention that this was Mark's third pass at taking the bar exam.

"He may be the newest addition to the legal staff," whispered Annie, "but he's been on the payroll for years."

"What!" Annie kept the books on the hourly employees.

"Sure, since college."

"He went to college in South Carolina. How could he have been working here?"

"Exactly."

"… and I know that next year will be even better. I'm sure you'll all be happy with your checks next week."

"The usual fifty this year? Or does he mean seventy-five?" Annie speculated. I was the only female partner in an all-male family firm, although in November they had hired three youngsters fresh out of law school, one of whom was my new assistant, Kim.

I targeted the party platters, rationalizing that at five-foot-nine, I could distribute the fat grams over a greater area than most.

"Good work on *Burnham*, Emma." Mr. McCook was spearing roast beef. "Ed says you were a big help with the settlement negotiations." Ed had contributed absolutely nothing on that file.

"That's good to hear. Thank you."

"You've moved a great many cases in the last year or so. I want you to know that it is much appreciated." Mr. McCook was a charming old gentleman, unlike his son Ed, who was a pompous ass.

I positioned myself by the punch bowl and Kim hove alongside. I filled her glass and asked if she was enjoying her new job.

"I am most of the time. David said something to me last week." Oh, no. "I was in the little kitchen on the first floor, and he came up behind me and asked if I liked to cook. In kind of a strange voice. I said that I usually get take-out and left quickly. Don't you think that's weird?"

"Very. I'll speak to his father about it." David was the elder of Mr. McCook's sons and a notorious womanizer.

"I'd appreciate it. I really like it here… otherwise."

My Book Club met once a month. That night, we discussed Hemingway's *A Moveable Feast*, his memoir of Paris after World War I, where he was an intimate of expatriates James Joyce, Gertrude Stein and F. Scott Fitzgerald. In October, we had read a series of essays on the women of the same period—Stein and Colette, among others.

"Interesting when you compare the two," Eliot said after an hour of discussion. Eliot was a law school classmate.

"Do you mean the two books, or the two groups?" Denise, another classmate, asked.

"Both. Boiled down to the bones, Hemingway's book is about men who drink, eat, gamble, and cheat on their wives. The Left Bank women, however, stayed together for decades and worked."

"That's *very* boiled down. Reread some of the language in Hemingway. Deceptively simple. Almost poetry," said Dottie. Dottie was a paralegal in Nick's firm.

"These women were hardly chaste," Denise said. "They took huge social risks. Look at Colette."

"I love what Hemingway writes in the very beginning about drinking cold white wine, and eating oysters," I said. "How they taste like the sea. Doesn't that passage make you want to fly to Paris right now?"

Eliot flipped her short bleached hair for effect.

"This is Connecticut, Emma. We have vast quantities of oysters and white wine."

"Yes, but aren't you lulled by the repetitions? Cold and sea and taste?"

"I'm disgusted by the fact that, although he decided that he didn't have enough money for wood to keep warm, he *was* able to buy his succulent oysters. Look at the last few pages, when he starts to cheat on his wife, how he talks about it as *her* trick, an act of fate. Anything but being a weak weasel. He claims that it all began in innocence. The man's a jerk!"

"Well, I think we've covered the Left Bank sufficiently. Shall we try Bloomsbury next time? Or perhaps a classic? How about an Austen?" Jane was a high school English teacher and very skillful at reining us in.

"How about *Persuasion*, which is my favorite. Or *Emma*?"

Dottie grinned. "I've always wanted to know, Em. Why your first name?"

"Flaubert. *Madame Bovary.*"

"But Emma Bovary was a shallow, material woman who was never satisfied with any aspect of her life," Jane said.

"Precisely."

"She drives her husband to despair. She commits suicide!"

"Nevertheless. These are qualities that would appeal to Audrey."

"So, shall we read *Persuasion*? Good. Austen it will be." If Jane had a gavel she would bang it.

On Friday night, Nick spoke to Doug, still in Boston, from the library. I placed big vases of holly and greens about the house. I hung garland and red bows from the banisters. I wrapped the last of the presents and arranged them under the tree. I planned the menu. I unearthed my calligraphy pen and worked on place cards for the dinner table. Finally, Nick made his report.

"Doug says that he would prefer not to be with your family on holidays. He would like it to be just the four of us together. He's uncomfortable around your mother. I couldn't get him to commit to anything. He's calling Deborah now." It was impossible to discern whether Nick was condoning this nonsense or merely too exhausted to react.

"Why did he agree to the plan that we proposed back in November?"

"I think he was afraid to tell me how he felt."

"If Doug was a twelve-year-old boy and you were newly divorced, I could accept this. But he's a graduate student and you've been divorced for years. He isn't MY family, after all. Why should I want to be alone with YOUR kids for my holidays?"

"I'm sure he has never looked at the situation from your perspective."

"But I'm invariably expected to consider it from his."

"Look, don't worry about this, Emma. It will work out. I have to go to bed."

I called my sister Kate from my study. "Have you spoken to Audrey?" she asked.

"Now what?"

"She's concerned about snow. She thinks we should have a storm plan, as in picking her up earlier so she isn't stranded on the twenty-fourth. Tom thinks we should just leave her in Ridgefield."

"In case of a storm or in general?"

"He didn't say. He did mention that he's planning to be pickled from alcohol next week."

"Why?"

"He's afraid he'll kill her."

"Hmm. Is there anything else?"

"She wants to visit Dad's grave."

"We can't even FIND Dad's grave."

"We brought up the headstone issue again. Tom told her that we're going to bury her exactly the same way she buried Dad."

"With a free footer from the Veterans' Administration?"

"Except that she didn't serve."

"Right. Well, let me know what I can do. I have the yearly Douglas Drama going on here, and Nick is refusing to cope."

"New girlfriend? I'll call you next week."

Denise called just as I was leaving the office that afternoon.

"Did you get the email on mediation training?" she asked. "It's being offered by the Connecticut Alliance of Mediation and Collaborative Professionals. I think I'm going to do it."

"I saw it. They're doing a dinner program in a couple of weeks on handling crazy clients. Sounds like a talk that I can't afford to miss. Why do you want to train as a mediator?"

"I like the idea of helping people to settle their own problems."

I laughed. "Imagine never having to set foot in a courtroom again!"

"Yes! No more wasted time, no more senseless battles over nothing, no more registered nasty-grams from other lawyers."

"You've talked me into it! I'll get certified with you. I've always felt that litigation was a complete waste of time and money. I'd really like to see my practice move in a different direction."

Denise laughed. "So would I! A different direction that includes more time, more money, and less stress!"

That night, I dreamed that I'm back at Vanderbilt University, ready to start my senior year. I have English Literature in five minutes, I haven't bought the required books, and I'm frantic because I don't know where the class is supposed to be meeting.

Then, I'm climbing up a ladder to my law firm, which is located through a trap door in the ceiling. Our managing partner is howling at his secretary because he can't find his stapler.

Finally, I'm driving up a long, winding mountain path that seems to go on forever. I have to dodge around large rocks and other natural debris. At the top of the mountain is a beautiful new law school, with a fountain in the courtyard and a huge, airy library. I sit down and pull a gold pen and a purple legal pad out of my briefcase.

The Sunday before Christmas, I could no longer contain myself.

"What's the story, Nick? Have we come to an understanding with your kids?"

"Define understanding."

"Do I know how many people will be here for dinner on Christmas Eve?"

"No, not yet."

"When do you expect to obtain this information, counselor?"

"I'm calling them tonight. Deborah's already here, staying with Liz."

"She's two miles away and you're going to discuss this *on the phone*?"

"She knows that you're angry, so she doesn't want to come here, and I'm certainly not going there."

"Why not meet somewhere neutral? I need to go food shopping, you know. Tenderloins don't just drop down the chimney. Nor does Büche de Noel."

"Where do you suggest?" I had to make these decisions, and they were his kids.

"There are about twenty restaurants in town. Pick one."

I charged upstairs to the Hunt Room to start preparing for Audrey's arrival. I had named our three guest rooms, to deter Nick from referring to them as Deborah's or Doug's. I had brass plates made up for each door. I was sure that our friends felt that this was pretentious. I preferred to think of it as defiance.

Macduff, our Welsh Terrier, perched in the armchair while I made the bed. Audrey had claimed that she favored the Hunt Room over the Rose Room, as the latter had only one and a half windows and was therefore claustrophobic. Recalling this, I tucked in her sheets extra tightly. I heard Nick shout from the front hall: "We're meeting at The Grill in fifteen minutes." Splendid. Perhaps I'd actually be able to finalize my dinner plans. "Make sure there's no more nonsense about taking stands," I hollered back.

Ten minutes after he left, there was a loud knock on the front door. Our new neighbor from across the street was standing without, bearing gifts.

"Woo hoo! Harrod's!"

"I remembered that you enjoyed your trip to London." Clifford was from Bath, but had relocated over here to avoid the British press. Our news media had yet to discover Warwick on the map.

"Please, come in. I'm sorry that you've just missed Nick."

"Thanks, but no time." Clifford was eyeing Mac, who was eyeing the food basket. "Lovely sporting Welsh you have there. Big, isn't he?"

"One of my recurrent nightmares is that he gets bigger! Do you hunt when you're home?"

"Not any longer. I had to give up my horses after the trial. Legal fees, you know."

"Yes, ah, oh." Extreme embarrassment. "Well, thank you so much. I know that we'll all enjoy this." Four ounces of caviar!

I contemplated an entire day with Doug, Deborah, and Audrey. I pulled out my holiday cookbook and located the champagne punch recipe.

Nick made an appearance at about ten, and I watched him mix a double martini.

"Well, I talked to Deborah." My husband had a genius for stating the obvious. "What's this basket?"

"I'll tell you later. Was anything accomplished?"

"Oh, wow, smoked oysters."

"NICK!"

"She started crying. She said that she knows you don't like her." True. "She said that you roll your eyes at her all the time." Woops. "She said that she's tried to be friends with you and she doesn't know what else to do. She was really very upset." I'll bet she was.

"But it didn't occur to her that the fact that she and her brother ruin my holidays every year might have SOME bearing on how I feel about her?"

"She says she just wants you to be a part of the family, Emma."

"Can't you tell when you're being manipulated? She's trying to drive a wedge between us and you're letting her."

"You manipulate me all the time."

"Wrong. I coerce. Totally different."

"Speaking of coercion, where's Abby? I hear growling."

"She ate the corner off the family room bookcase, so I banished her to the bathroom. What about dinner?"

"They're both coming at noon, and Doug is bringing Sara down Tuesday night, so she'll be here, as well. Deborah said that they both want relations between us to be better." No doubt they also wanted their Christmas checks.

"Terrific. So, that makes it the five of us, plus Kate, Tom, Hannah, and Audrey. I thought that Doug doesn't like spending holidays with my family."

"Probably Sara's being here changes that. I think he's serious about her."

"They've been dating for how long? Three months?" This was a record for Doug.

"Just try to be nice."

"I'm always nice."

"And watch the eye rolling."

Two hours later, I had purchased the necessary comestibles and was cramming them into the two refrigerators, when the phone rang. Doug.

"Hi, Emma. I'm in a jam."

"DON'T tell me you're not coming to dinner tomorrow."

"That's not it. It's Mom. She's having my grandmother and my aunt and uncle, besides having Deborah. So, there are no bedrooms left. She won't let Sara and me share a room anyway, and she won't let us drink in her house. I thought that since you have three empty rooms…."

"Two. My mother is staying with us."

"Oh. It would only be for two nights."

"Fine. When can we expect you tonight?"

"About seven. Thanks for this, Emma."

I pitched a set of sheets on the bed in the Rose Room and called Nick.

"That's terrific, Em! It means he feels comfortable enough to stay with us."

"It means that he can't keep his hands to himself for two lousy nights, and he knows we'll allow it. Why doesn't Liz permit drinking in her house?"

"She thinks my father was an alcoholic and she's afraid it will run in the family."

"*Was* he an alcoholic?"

"No. But she gives Doug such a hard time when he drinks in front of her that he feels it's easier not to."

"How lucky for us."

Doug and Sara arrived at eight-fifteen. We had already had dinner, but I warmed some beef stew for them. Doug was a big athletic type, attractive until he opened his mouth. Sara was from the south shore of Boston. Used to money, and extremely self confident.

Doug went into the refrigerator for another beer.

"How about some more music?" Nick had a terrific collection of old jazz records.

"Could you turn it *down*, Dad? It's really *loud*." After a pause, Nick did.

I decided that it was time to start working on the dressing. Peeling chestnuts can take hours. Hopefully.

Our guests having retired, Nick and I sat in the living room, looking at the tree and savoring his special brandy. I love to watch the reflections of the colored bulbs on the ceiling. They're magical.

"So what do you think of her?"

"I think she's too mature for him, but maybe she sees something in Doug that I don't."

"You're always so hard on him. He's a good kid and he means well."

"I'd like to see him act like a man and not like a big entitled weenie. He should be grateful for the way he was raised. He never seems to appreciate how lucky he was. How lucky he *is*."

"You have bad memories of Christmas and you can't let go of that."

"I have bad memories of one Christmas in particular. My dear daddy dropped dead ten years ago tomorrow, if you recall, so how about cutting me a little slack?"

We sat quietly for a while. Mac curled up between us on the love seat.

Suddenly, there was a shout, a heavy thud, and the sound of running feet. Mac sat up, barked once, and took off for parts unknown.

"Get her, get her." Doug was screaming like—I hate to say it—a woman.

"WHAT IS IT?" I had no patience with hysteria.

"That bitch! She wet me."

"What!"

"She jumped on the bed and took a WHIZ on me!"

I gulped down a laugh. Not successfully. Nick had already run upstairs and collected the furry fiend. Over the sound of Doug's blubbering, one could discern the voice of Abby, registering defiance.

"Do you have something else to wear? If not, you can borrow from your dad." Was it possible for terriers to get coal in their stockings?

Once Abs had been contained and Doug sent back to bed, we resumed our positions in the living room.

"I hope this is not a precursor for tomorrow," I said, only half kidding.

The library clock chimed midnight.

It was Christmas Eve.

CHAPTER THREE

Step Children

Early the next morning, I had the table set, the flowers arranged, the vegetables washed and cut, and the base for the champagne punch chilling in the refrigerator. The terriers had been walked and fed, and Abby was deposited on our four-poster with Nick, who probably wouldn't descend for hours. There was nary a sound from our guests in the Rose Room. Mac and I were basking in a halo of organizational efficiency.

It was close to eleven when I came in from cutting more holly for the sideboard. Nick was presiding over the coffee maker, and Sara and Doug were consuming scrambled eggs. Macduff circled in hopes of scraps. There was still no sign of Abby.

Sara followed me into the dining room.

"Deborah called. She is going to be stopping by a friend's house before dinner. She may be late." And so it began. "Also, your little dog got into the bathroom after my shower and ripped a hole in my bath towel. So I let her keep it." This explained the frenzied tearing noises that were emanating from our bedroom.

"I hope you weren't wearing it at the time!"

"Well, I was almost dry anyway."

Nick was pouring me an ice coffee.

"All four fireplaces are set to go, Em. Which bottles of wine do you want brought up?" Nick's contribution to any gathering at our home was invariably limited to fire and alcohol.

Kate, Tom, Hannah, and Audrey arrived at one. Hannah tore through the family room, kitchen, and dining room, accelerated as she passed across the front hall and into the living room, and came to a halt in front of the tree. "NOT YET!" shrieked her mother from the kitchen, and the danger was averted.

Audrey was in the dining room scrutinizing my table arrangements. "You have me seated next to your stepson, dear. It is protocol to place me at Nick's right, as the most important female guest. Your flowers are too tall, dear. They will block conversation across the table. Why are the champagne glasses out?"

"We are celebrating Kate's promotion, Mother. Deborah will be seated next to her father, as it puts her as far as possible away from me. And the flowers are fine. Anything else?"

"I hope you don't think I'm being critical, dear. You're too sensitive."

Tom went straight for the single malt. I was tempted to join him. Audrey had cornered Sara by the hors d'oeuvres table; Mac was hovering around same, while Hannah pulled on his tail; Nick and Doug were in animated discussion about something, no doubt sports-related.

Deborah made her entrance at three o'clock. As always, she was the picture of poise. She smiled graciously and immediately took over the room. Nick shot me a look that said "Behave!" as I hung up her coat and brought her gifts into the living room. Deborah, a healthy blond, was wearing a very short, navy blue dress, and when she sat down there was so much exposed thigh, one was forced to instantly avert the eyes. If someone had told her that she could successfully carry off such an ensemble, she was misinformed.

"The house looks wonderful, Emma," breathed Miss Congeniality. "The flowers are glorious, and I love what you've done with the holly."

The cocktail hour had officially commenced. I had availed myself of my neighbor's bounty and all was appreciated. I was feeling slightly mollified after two glasses of champagne punch, and tossed Macduff a cocktail shrimp. Hannah sat on the floor by the tree with a determined expression. Deborah took over the conversation in her airy, phony voice, interrupting at least two people.

"So, Lauren has just gotten engaged, Dad." Knowing full well that most of us present neither knew, nor cared, about the identity of said Lauren. "Her father is arranging for a fabulous reception at one of those mansions in Westchester." Uh oh. I caught Kate's eye. Where was this going?

"Really?" Nick replied. "Anyone I know?"

"Jack Coombs from Greenwich. You remember. They dated back in high school. And Tara just got pinned for Christmas. They'll probably be engaged by graduation."

"That's nice, honey."

"Tara says her dad is thrilled about it and is already talking about the wedding he'll give her."

"Got anyone in mind for yourself, Deborah?" I looked straight at her. She drew back a tad, but managed to maintain the plastic smile. Skills well developed for one so young.

"Oh, no. I just thought Dad would be interested."

I made my escape to start the wild rice. Kate followed me and refilled her glass.

"Now what is she up to?"

"She obviously wanted her dad to jump in and tell her all about the fabulous nuptial that he has been considering for her since birth."

"She's a planner, I'll give her that. And she certainly knows how to work her father."

Tom was clearly proud of Kate's promotion. "She's only been with them for five years and this is the third time. They know she's irreplaceable."

"No one is irreplaceable, Tom, dear," Audrey said. "After all, look what happened to you."

"That was a personality problem, Mother, and you know it." Kate looked ferocious.

"Exactly, dear. One must learn to work with others in a corporate setting, mustn't one? Especially when one has responsibilities at home. How lucky for you, Tom, dear, that our Kate is so successful, and you didn't have to worry on that score." Tom got up for more Scotch. Kate seethed. Hannah started poking boxes.

"Tom is doing very well at his new company, Mother."

"I'm sure that's so, dear. It's just too bad that he had to take a reduction in pay to find a position."

Kate and I again sought refuge in the kitchen. I combined several herbs with olive oil and proceeded to brush the mixture over the tenderloin. Kate speared the boiling potatoes in a purposeful manner.

"You've done a great job with this kitchen, Em. Huge improvement over the original gold and avocado green."

"Thanks. The real victory was convincing Nick to spend the money."

"You always do that!"

"What?"

"Respond to a compliment about this house with an attack on Nick. You have such a nice life! Two lovely homes, a fancy car, a talented horse, a career, and the time to do whatever you want. Do you realize how shallow you sound when you make fun of Nick?"

I tipped my champagne glass toward her. "Merry Christmas to you too, little sister. If I was looking for abuse in my own home, I'd be having this delightful chat with Audrey instead."

"Look, I remember how rough your first marriage was; how poor you were. So why don't you appreciate how you live now?"

"Because I have little to no say regarding any part of my so-called great life. Nick hoards what he makes and I have no access to it. My salary draw as a new partner, after taxes, and health insurance, pays for my expenses, and that's about it. It's a constant battle to keep my credit cards down, and I have very little savings." I took a big gulp of champagne. "Nick never misses the chance to remind me how expensive Joy is. He knows damn well I couldn't afford her on my own. I feel trapped." I drained my glass, and took another bottle of champagne from the refrigerator.

"How many glasses is that now, Em?" Kate asked, quietly.

"Would you kindly get off this mothering kick? I've been taking care of myself for quite some time without your help, thanks. Without anybody's help, actually."

"As far as I can see, you're anesthetizing yourself. You're either exhausted from your schedule, or drinking. What has happened to you? In law school you were a ball of fire; you were going to make a fortune and change the world. Now you seem stuck in a career that isn't paying you what you're worth, and you don't like doing it."

Hannah bounced into our midst.

"Mommy, Daddy is waving a knife at Grandma."

"Oh, Lord!" Kate sprinted toward the door. "Listen, Emma. Dad dropped dead ten years ago today. I asked Audrey. Dad's father and grandfather were abusive alcoholics too. Just don't carry on in his place, OK? Please."

Doug appeared. "Someone needs to put more logs on the fire in the library."

Deborah emerged from the powder room. "Emma, Mom always kept the heat on high in that room, so the pipes wouldn't freeze."

Dinner was served at four-thirty. I seated Kate and Tom on either side of me, with Hannah propped up in a booster chair. Sara helped pass serving dishes while Nick carved. Doug wanted soda with dinner. Tom was clearly toasted.

"The meat is a little *pink*, dear," Audrey said.

"It's *supposed* to be, Mother," Kate replied through her teeth.

After dessert, we released Hannah, who scampered off in the direction of presents.

Kate and Sara helped me clear up. The men stayed in the living room with Ms. Always Right holding court. I caught a glimpse of her standing by the fireplace, arm draped along the mantel. Audrey wandered in and leaned on the counter. "You missed a spot," she informed Sara, who was drying.

Kate got her family's belongings together and they departed. It was agreed that we would keep Audrey another night and bring her to Kate's for Christmas Day. "For her own protection," grumbled Tom.

That night, I dreamed that I'm in the room that looks like our childhood bedroom in the Brooklyn apartment, except that there is a fireplace in one wall. I build up the fire and it starts to burn well. Then, Kate points out that a bird is hatching from its egg, right by the fire. I pick it up and move it to safety. There's a cat after the little bird. I scoop up the cat, and it sticks its claws into my arm. I hand the cat to Kate. Then, I notice that the baby chick is a tiny human being, walking around on its new legs.

On the morning of the twenty-sixth, we tossed the terriers into Nick's Volvo and proceeded north. Nick had owned the house on Pequot Lake in New Hampshire since his first wife's administration. He graduated from Dartmouth College and had never missed a reunion, a homecoming, or a home ice hockey game. I could recite two verses of the Dartmouth alma mater, but wouldn't even recognize the first line of my own.

The deck, which had a good view of the lake, was buried under about two feet of snow, and the house was bitterly cold. I checked all the rooms on three floors, turning up the thermostats. Nick went down to the basement to turn on the water. We cranked up the wood stove on the main level and uncorked the chardonnay. I took the brie out of the cooler. Peace.

"Which room do you want to put Doug and Sara?"

"I beg your pardon?"

"They'll be here tomorrow morning, Em. Remember, I told you that they were coming up to ski?"

We were assembling our ski gear when Doug and Sara arrived.

"Did you get us ski passes, Dad?"

"You are supposed to buy your own lift tickets, like the rest of humanity," I replied, and immediately was the recipient of one of Nick's special looks.

"But I'm a grad student. I don't have much money."

"Then why did you invite yourself? We've had this plan for months." An ominous snarl was developing in my voice. Sara jumped in.

"I have plenty of cash, Doug. Let's drop our bags in our room and go."

"I hate this room. There's no view." They disappeared.

Pequot Mountain was a good local ski area and had become popular, despite competition from the much larger mountains across the river in Vermont. I was not an accomplished skier, and prudence dictated that I took a few runs on the beginner trails before joining the others. The men and Sara departed for the high speed lift. Ah, freedom.

I proceeded in a leisurely fashion down the easiest trail. Two boys on snowboards flew by. A father, skiing backward, was towing his young daughter just ahead of me. Four toddlers passed me, giggling. They didn't have poles.

God this was humiliating. I had only been skiing a few years and, therefore, lacked the courageous arrogance that comes with learning a sport as a child.

By three o'clock, I began to experience muscle fatigue. "Oh, one more run," begged Nick. "You're doing much better on the intermediate trails this time."

The lift was approaching the drop-off point, our tips were up, and I was collecting my poles when Nick shouted down to his friend Pete on the trail below us. I looked down, failing to notice as I did so that Nick had crossed his left ski over my right one. There was nothing I could do. Nick was safely off, while I had missed the spot to disembark. The lift moved upward and I jumped, landing in a heap in a snowdrift. The lifts halted and the attendant came running out to assist me. "I *told* you that I was too tired," I barked to Nick.

Pete and Jane were up at their place across the lake, and we invited them over for dinner. Although they had been friends with Liz when she was married to Nick, Jane and I had connected quickly, and I had asked her to join my Book Club.

Jane had brought her famous double baked potatoes.

"Doug wants to watch the game," Nick mentioned nervously.

"Not happening, Nick."

"Why?"

"Because the TV is in the middle of the living room, and we have a house full of people." Nick knew damn well how I'd react; he just wanted to pass off the problem, leaving me to be the bad guy.

Doug sulked and disappeared into their room.

I sent Nick out to the deck to grill swordfish in twenty degree weather.

Jane was telling us a real hair-raiser about the night before her mother died.

"It wasn't a dream. Someone grabbed my arm and shook it, hard. I was too terrified to scream. I know it was my father, trying to warn me about Mom."

"Tell them about the cups, Emma," said Nick.

"A few months after my dad died, we gave a dinner party at home. I was alone in the kitchen and had lined up the coffee cups and saucers on the counter. I turned to get the cream out of the refrigerator, and when I looked back, one cup and saucer was on the other side of the counter. No one had come into the room, and there hadn't been an earthquake."

"You think it was your dad?" Pete asked.

"Let's just say that I haven't dismissed the possibility. It would be just like him. And there is so much that can't be explained by modern science. I think it's just ignorance to assume that we have all the answers." Also, it had scared the hell out of me.

The next morning, Jane and I put on snowshoes and went for a walk on the lake. The ice was about two feet thick, and there were fishing huts and cross-country skiers dotted across the terrain. One intrepid soul had an ice boat. The blades made an eerie slicing sound. Jane continually poked the snow with her ski poles. The ice would occasionally groan and crack, which for some reason made me nervous.

"Have you had any time to read, Emma?"

"I did reread *Persuasion* for our next meeting. I'm also about a third of the way through an excellent biography of Prince Albert. Brilliant man."

"Queen Victoria has always been one of your passions, hasn't she? If passion is the right word."

"Yes, but I am most interested in the years that they were together. After his death, she became rather odd."

"She was a woman who was greatly influenced by the men in her life. I have always felt that while she was a good queen, with a strong sense of duty, what we call the Victorian Age was largely the product of her husband's efforts."

"And isn't it difficult, as women, to admit that!"

"I amuse myself by comparing her to Eleanor Roosevelt."

"She is another of my pet subjects! Which astounds Nick, by the way. He insists that the Roosevelts were Socialists."

"It was Eleanor's strength that was so attractive. You don't have to agree with her politics to admire her work, or her character."

"Jane, do you mind if I ask you about Nick's marriage to Liz?"

"Of course not. As long as I'm not expected to betray a confidence."

"No, this is more of a question about your observations. Did you feel as though Nick valued Liz's contributions to their marriage?"

Jane paused. "In a word, no. It is very clear that Nick does not value the concept of home, or the effort that goes into making one's home a place of peace, or beauty. I've often heard him say that housework isn't work, nor is raising children. In my opinion, Nick feels that money is the only real measure of contribution, to anything."

"Was he controlling with money then, too?"

"Much worse, frankly. Liz was a grade school teacher, and she gave it up when Doug was born. Thank goodness she decided to get her realtor's license later on, or I don't know what she would have done. She never even had a credit card when they were married. Just a joint checking account, and there were only funds available there when Nick felt like depositing them."

"I had no idea! No wonder Deborah is always after him about money."

"I have a feeling that Deborah has a foot in two camps: she wants to avenge her mother, but she also wants to maintain her father's good opinion, as he is the one with the cash."

"What about Doug?"

"Doug was always considered the disappointment, but I wonder if a lot of that had to do with the fact that Doug never played up to Nick. He wanted his Dad to love him and pay attention to him, and that was his agenda. Laudatory, really, considering his sister's antics."

"I agree. But I don't believe having his father and his younger sister fix all of his mistakes is the answer either."

"No, but that's been the family pattern. Even Liz works that shift, if you'll pardon the colloquialism."

"Thanks Jane, I appreciate it."

"I've said too much, but I trust you. Liz doesn't have your personality. You strike me, Emma, as a woman who ultimately gets everything that she is after."

"Yes. The question is, however, whether I've ever really wanted what I get."

CHAPTER FOUR

Narcissistic Personality Disorder

"What do you think so far?" Denise asked. It was the lunch break during mediation training, and as usual, I was first in line to collect my tuna wrap and ice tea.

"This stuff is a little too touchy-feely for me. All the terms: reframe, buy-in, normalizing, no resistance. I feel as though I'm back at a sorority retreat, and I hated those weekends."

"There's a bit much in terms of kinder and softer, I agree." Denise put some pasta salad on her plate, and grabbed a roll. "But it's all common sense really. Most conflicts arise from a place of fear—fear of a loss of some kind. Everyone can resonate with that. Once all the fears are on the table, I imagine the process of mediation can be quite powerful."

"Definitely. I can't tell you how often I've had couples in my conference room screaming with rage at each other, and the problem was something simple, like he's afraid of losing his kids, or she's afraid the new girlfriend will take over with them. When everyone is calmed down and assured, civility returns."

"This seems to be a whole new language. We're neutral facilitators, not advocates. We're supposed to make our clients feel safe, and welcome, while remaining in charge of the process. I like that mediation is about presenting options to people, not steamrolling them into submission."

"And no rulings! I never understood the difference between mediation and arbitration before, but now I get it. Arbitration is fake court. Someone makes a decision. In mediation, the parties make the decisions, and we help them get there."

We sat by the window near a group of therapists. One woman was complaining about the fact that while the attorney mediators were allowed to practice what sounds like therapy, anyone who was not a lawyer was forbidden to draft a contract.

"Lawyers always work it so they're stealing the show," she grumbled to her colleague.

Denise and I grinned at each other.

"I know how you feel about talk therapy, Em," Denise whispered.

"Hey, if people want to wallow in their pasts like bugs in a cesspool, who am I to keep them from such delights? And if they want to spend thousands doing it for five years or more, without any discernable results, I wish them the best. Throw in some anti depressants to keep them in an emotional coma, so they can get through the day. The only people who benefit from that nonsense are the therapists. And the drug companies." I munched on my chocolate chip cookie. "But I'm open to trying mediation. It's focusing on the future, which sounds sensible. I'm all about seeing the practical side of things."

"People should make these agreements before their marriage disintegrates," Denise noted. "Or better yet, before they get married."

"A whole new line on pre-nups and post-nups! I like it! I'd so much rather keep couples together than help them find ways to live apart."

Denise got up and took our plates to the tray in the corner. "Well, hold on to that thought. We're going to spend the rest of the afternoon doing role plays."

"Oh no!" I yipped. "I hate fake drama. It's even worse than the real thing. At least with the sorority they let us sing a lot."

"Well, not today. Just don't hit anyone, all right?"

Annie buzzed me the next day before I had hung up my coat.

"Ed would like you to join him in his office."

"What's up?"

"New client. Husband in a post-divorce custody battle. Ed wants you in on the meeting."

After the obligatory handshake with the new Mr. Ambrose, I took a seat in one of the Tulane armchairs in Ed's office.

"John and his wife were divorced in Stamford two years ago. They share joint custody of their two young children. He lives in Darien, she lives in New Canaan. He commutes to the city."

So far, the classic Fairfield County scenario.

"Pursuant to their separation agreement, John has the children every other weekend, as well as every Wednesday night, plus the usual holidays—Father's Day and so forth. This arrangement was working reasonably well until this past fall."

"How old are the children, Mr. Ambrose?"

"Tucker is four and Charlotte is two and a half."

"The problem," continued Ed, "is as follows. Early on a Saturday morning in October, John picked the children up at their mother's for a scheduled weekend visitation. He then received an emergency call on his cell from the office and was immediately forced to drive into Manhattan."

"Did the children go with you?"

"My grandmother stays with me at the house, so I dropped the kids off with her."

Ed registered discomfort.

"She often looks after them for me when I have to be some-where quickly," Ambrose said.

Ed squirmed in his chair yet again. What was the catch?

"Patty, my ex-wife, happened to call the house to remind me about Tucker's swim class, and Tucker answered the phone. So now we are back in court. Patty wants sole custody."

I assumed that I'd missed something relevant.

"Patty, you see, did not know about my grandmother."

"How long has your grandmother been babysitting for you?"

"Since the divorce. The children love her, but Patty didn't know about it," Ambrose repeated.

"She doesn't like your grandmother?"

"She's never met her."

"Why hasn't your ex-wife met your grandmother?"

"Because she died when I was eight."

Aha. The catch.

Ed rejoined the conversation. "John's former counsel has declined to continue representing him. So, here we are."

Of course I was handed this file. Not at gun point, but the sensation was similar.

I woke up at four a.m. the next morning, breathing hard. I had dreamed that a man gets into my Audi, puts it into reverse, and bashes it several times into the front of the car behind it. A voice next to me says, "Fix your red car."

Joy and I worked on counter-cantering during our next lesson. That is to say, I did. Joy wanted nothing to do with the concept. Finally she reared up and refused to move forward.

"You're on her mouth too much," Jeannie said. "If you don't give her any leg, she has nowhere to go but up. Try pushing your shoulders back and use your core stomach muscles to hold them in place. You're hunched over her neck, and it's pissing her off."

"OK, I'll try."

"How about a 'shoulder in' down the long side?"

But Joy kept pulling into the center of the ring. My legs were screaming from the effort.

"I'll get on her tomorrow," Jeannie said. "Just finish up with a canter in both directions. There's no sense in fighting with her."

We executed a couple of perfect flying lead changes, which lifted my spirits somewhat.

I walked Joy back to her barn and unbuckled her girth. I put my gear in my tack trunk and retrieved the treat bag. I gave Joy her apple, which she ate from my hand in four ladylike bites. She rubbed her nose on my shoulder to express appreciation.

Denise and I carpooled to the New Haven Tennis Club for the dinner talk on crazy clients.

"Have you heard of this female who's speaking?" I asked, reading the program email as Denise navigated through rush hour traffic on I-95. "Crystelle Shields, LMFT."

"You'll like her," Denise replied. "She's a psychotherapist who is passionate about steering patients away from shrinks and drugs. She believes in integrative health: energy work, a body in balance, as well as talk therapy."

"Finally! I'm so tired of being practically the only one I know who isn't on some form of medication."

"Do you think the people in this country will ever figure out that they're being duped by the drug companies? And that the doctors buy into the deception because they need the constant patient traffic to meet their huge overheads?"

"Which in turn are controlled by the insurance companies? It would take a miracle."

The Connecticut Alliance of Mediation and Collaborative Professionals (CAMCP) had been founded about eight years before by a small group of financial planners, therapists, and lawyers, whose mission was to make a difference in the divorce process in Connecticut. Their message was growing, as were their numbers. Denise and I had signed on as general members, with a promise to be certified in mediation and collaborative practice within a year.

Crystelle Shields was introduced as dessert was served.

"Rather than stand here and give you a lecture on mental illness straight from the Diagnostic and Statistical Manual of Mental Disorders, or DSM-IV," she began, "let's try something different. Show of hands—who here has seen the movie *Gaslight*, with Ingrid Bergman and Charles Boyer?"

About half the occupants of the room laughed and raised their hands in the air. Denise and I looked at each other and shrugged.

"For those of you who haven't had the pleasure, the basic plot is as follows: Paula meets Gregory in Italy and, after a speedy romance, marries him and returns to Victorian London with him to live in the house that she inherited from her wealthy aunt. Gregory is charming and attentive, seemingly the perfect husband. However, the reality is that Gregory is surreptitiously and relentlessly breaking down Paula's self esteem, to the point that she is completely isolated from the outside world and convinced that she is losing her mind."

Shields paused. "Show of hands again. How many of you have heard of Narcissistic Personality Disorder?" All of the therapists and a smattering of lawyers raised their hands.

"I have just described to you what happens to a woman who is married to a man who has NPD."

"Oh my God!" muttered Denise.

"The sad truth is that these men—and it almost always *is* men—are attracted to women who start out as vibrant, productive members of society. Often these women have fulfilling careers and are loving, caring and supportive individuals. Check back with them in ten years, however, and the picture is very different. The same women are now doubting whether they are capable of bagging groceries at the local market.

"To the outside world, a man with NPD presents as a charming, thoughtful, and very often successful person. He may appear to be loving and generous to his wife in public. Unfortunately, these people are accomplished actors who know that they are empty frauds inside. They are incapable of conducting a real relationship at any level, because they are unable to feel empathy, or intimacy. A person with NPD is arrogant, self absorbed, and convinced that he is Master of the Universe. He tends to monopolize conversations, and the focus is all about him. He takes the credit for everything, and the blame for nothing. His greatest fear is being discovered. Secretly, he is consumed by anger and self loathing, and he hates anyone who is capable of real love and intimacy. Once a spouse does uncover his act, he will ruthlessly destroy her.

"How does this personality disorder begin? As children, people with NPD tend to have over-sensitive temperaments, which are compounded by either over-indulgence by the parents, or child abuse. The behavior manifests in early adulthood.

"How does it feel to be in a marriage with a person who has NPD? In twenty-five years of practice, I have heard the same statement from clients over and over again: 'I feel a terrible, aching loneliness whenever I'm in the same room with him.'"

A financial planner with a perplexed look on her face raised her hand. "Why did she marry him in the first place, then? Denial?"

"Good question. Statistically, spouses of people with NPD were often victims of child abuse and, therefore, used to and attracted by so-called love relationships that keep them feeling off-balance emotionally. As any therapist in this room will tell you, people will continue to attract the same patterns of abuse as adults, unless and until they release their childhoods, and move on to emotionally healthy relationships.

"The wife of a man with NPD is usually younger, attractive, and accomplished to the point that she makes him look good when they're out together. She must be an asset to his self-image, because this marriage is nothing more than a business deal. He is very charming to her at first. He may even praise her in public. But he doesn't actually feel a word that he says; it is only a manipulation calculated to feed his own ego. The confusion starts when the spouses are home alone together, and the verbal put-downs begin. One client told me that she had repeated nightmares of being on the deck of the Titanic as it went into its death throes and ultimately sank. Another client described her husband as having 'nobody home inside.' She reported that trying to connect with him was like walking in the front door of his personal house, only to emerge out on the back porch.

"Consistently, husbands with NPD use domination and control as a method of keeping their wives down. Their tactics may take the form of verbal, economic, and even sexual abuse. Remember that these people feel nothing inside beyond rage. Sex is a chore, and withholding sexual relations, or belittling their spouses with painful or shaming sex, are common methods of chipping away at a woman's self-esteem. Their wives mean nothing to them."

One of the lawyers raised his hand. "What happens when the wife wants a divorce?"

"The mask drops entirely, and what you'll see can be nothing short of frightening. But first, I'd like to say hats off to the courageous woman who makes the first move to end the marriage. In my experience, most of them don't. They've had the life sucked out of them by the energy vampire who they've married. However, if you suspect that your client or patient is the spouse of a person with NPD, please make sure that she has every kind of support available to her. I don't care if she's a licensed engineer or a home-making mother of four; she has experienced emotional battering of the worst sort, in my opinion, because it is a category of abuse that leaves no visible scar. And the horror will only increase during the divorce process. Like Paula in *Gaslight*, the wife will appear to be the partner who is mentally ill, while her husband plays the suffering victim."

Another lawyer stood up. "The financial affidavits tell the truth, though. I just finished a divorce that was by far the worst case of economic abuse that I've ever encountered, and the wife had an MBA and many years of experience on Wall Street."

Shields nodded. "Let me read to you an excerpt from a deposition that was taken a few months ago. My client's husband is being deposed regarding the location of various assets, mainly gold.

"Question: But why not open several safe deposit boxes at the same bank, as opposed to going to so many different banks?

Answer: One of the main reasons was for security purposes. I didn't think it was a prudent idea to put all the coins in one bank because of things that might happen.

Question: What did you think might happen to the safe deposit boxes?

Answer: First of all, the government can seize safe deposit boxes. Banks can get into trouble. There could be burglaries. You can have civil disorder in this country that might lead to problems.

Question: What leads you to worry that the government might seize a box of yours?

Answer: What's going on in the world. That's why.

Question: Why would they target your box as opposed to my box?

Answer: They might target your box too.

Question: Was your wife aware of the magnitude of the coins that you were hiding?

Answer: I don't think so."

Shields continued. "I have two major points to make here. Please take note of this man's obvious paranoia, which is another symptom of NPD. These people are perpetually on stage, deceiving and betraying everyone around them. Therefore, they assume that everyone else is doing the same to them, and they are obsessed with planning their next move to confuse the enemy. Also, this man has just testified to having fooled his wife for years with the extent of the assets accumulated during the marriage. She had been afraid to file for divorce because he continually told her that they had no money. The woman was terrified of ending her life as a bag lady. In this next excerpt, the same husband is justifying the fact that he had no interest in paying off his wife's student loans:

Question: Did you make any attempts to pay the student loans off?

Answer: No, I didn't.

Question: Why not?

Answer: I just didn't. They weren't my loans.

Question: How was your wife supposed to have the money to pay them?

Answer: I don't know. I can't answer that.

Question: Well, if you weren't going to pay them, and you didn't have any joint accounts with your wife, and you weren't giving her money on a regular basis, how did you imagine that they would be paid?

Answer: She could have gone to work, made money, and paid them.

Question: But I thought you testified earlier that it was okay for her not to work because you were making more than enough money to pay for the expenses of your family?

Answer: That's the way she could have paid them. They weren't my responsibility.

Question: And why was it that you paid them all off last year?

Answer: She demanded that I did. She said that if I didn't pay them off, she would get a divorce.

Question: Was that your only consideration?

Answer: She said she would have a better attitude, behave better, if I paid off the loans.

Question: Did she have a better attitude?

Answer: No.

Question: Did she behave better?

Answer: No.

Question: And you're mad about it because she didn't hold up her end of the bargain and you did?

Answer: I wouldn't put it that way.

Question: Do you feel that there is anything that you did to contribute to the breakdown of your marriage?

Answer: From my standpoint, not really. I mean I treated her very well. She had a good lifestyle. We took a lot of trips, we have a beach house. She has a nice car. She could go to work or not work as she chose. I thought I treated her fine."

Someone let out a loud "WHEW!" and there was a moment of silence.

Shields smiled. "Questions?"

"Is it possible to mediate a divorce when one of the spouses has NPD?"

"In my opinion, no," Shields responded. "The husband would play the charm angle to woo the mediator, but once the financial picture became clear and he felt pressure to consider his wife's point of view, he would turn on the mediator and the process would fail."

"So the only answer is litigation?" Denise asked.

"I'm afraid so. That assumes that the husband accepts the ultimate authority of the judge's decision. The best scenario is for the wife to receive an asset division up front, so that she is free from periodic alimony and continued contact with her ex-husband. Remember that his weapons are domination and control. If there are kids involved, the situation can become truly horrible. Children of an NPD parent learn early on to play a specific role to stay in that parent's mirror image of perfection. This type of learned behavior can take a terrible toll." She paused. "And I must warn you; this family scenario often sets the stage for incest, usually between the father and a daughter. The mother, if she knows, feels powerless."

There was another moment of silence as we all processed this information.

"Does *Gaslight* end on a positive note?" one of the therapists asked.

"Yes!" Crystelle Shields replied. "Paula is saved in the nick of time by a friend who sees Gregory for who he really is. It is truly satisfying to watch the transformation that occurs once Paula realizes what has been happening to her. I feel that every emotionally battered woman should have such an epiphany."

That night, I dreamed that I'm looking at an open, dorm-size refrigerator. It is full of wrapped food of the kind that is found in a chef's salad: proteins and greens. Someone shuts the door, picks up the fridge, and puts it in a black SUV or truck. I try to follow in my car, but I reach an intersection and don't know which way to turn. I feel like it's to the left, but a young man in another black car points me in the opposite direction. I follow him and turn into a parking lot on a little bit of a rise.

I woke up, and checked the clock on my bedside table. It was three a.m., and Nick was snoring. I eventually drifted off to sleep again.

I'm in one of those high-end, "ye old colonial" shopping malls. I'm walking down a path in front of all the stores, commenting on how pretty the structure is. But the path is strewn with discarded retail items on either side, so it's hard to walk.

I woke when the alarm went off at seven, and decided that it was time to do some research.

At lunchtime, I drove to the nearest bookstore in Westport. I found several shelves full of books on dream analysis and bought two that were written by psychologists and three that were written by psychics. I ate my turkey on rye at my desk, while I perused my reference materials. Colors in dreams were very important. Black was indicative of transformation and deeper understanding. Red meant vitality, but could also be a warning. Intersections were usually emotional crossroads. Proteins and vegetables had to do with strength and new growth. So who was the guy in the black car? And did the parking lot have to do with life in general or my career, specifically? Modes of transportation were heavily symbolic, apparently. Cars represented how we were moving ahead in our lives. So who was smashing up my beloved Audi? Malls or markets were about choices, and the cluttered passage was probably what was in my head at the moment, and how this muddle was preventing me from moving forward. But where did I want to go? And how could I make it happen?

I made notes by the various relevant sections, and dated them.

According to one of the psychic authors, the symbols would be repeated until the dreamer realized their significance and resolved the issue or issues presented.

I submitted to a Saturday lunch date with Audrey and Kate in Ridgefield. Audrey would park her car only in the bank lot in the center of town. I picked her up there and brought her to the restaurant. Kate had already secured a table and was enjoying a large piece of bread dipped in herbed oil.

"Do you *really* think you should, dear?"

Kate scowled.

"Well, isn't this delightful? My two daughters taking time from their busy schedules to have lunch with their poor widowed mother." I ordered a glass of chardonnay from a passing waitress.

"Are you planning anything new for your garden this spring, Mom?"

"The catalogs should be out soon," Kate added.

"I *had* hoped to start a small climbing rose garden. Perhaps one of you will help me dig the holes. I will also need peat moss. I suppose I *could* have it delivered; it's *so* heavy."

"Yes, Mother."

"I've considered a new rock garden by the patio. But it is *so* dark on the left side. Perhaps one of you would care to help me thin out some of the bushes there."

"You could hire someone, Mom," Kate suggested.

"Oh, *no*, dear. One must be very careful when one lives on a fixed income."

"Hannah has a part in the school play," Kate said.

"What will she be?"

"A duck. They're doing a farm story. Hannah now quacks everywhere she goes."

"Are you making her costume?"

"I've started it. Her bill is bright orange felt."

"Will I be invited, dear?"

"Yes, of course, Mother."

The waitress reappeared. Kate eyed the rolled lasagna at the next table, but clearly thought better of it. I ordered the grilled vegetable salad with goat cheese.

"Well, I would just *love* the shrimp scampi, but it *is* a bit pricey."

"I'm buying, Mom," Kate said, exasperated.

"How lovely, dear. I'll have the scampi and a glass of champagne. Are your desserts good today?"

A few hours later, Nick walked into my study.

"Channel Eight news just called," he said. "They want to talk to us about Clifford."

CHAPTER FIVE

Incest

Our road was lined with television crew vans by eight the next morning. The contents of one, a petite brunette with a microphone and accompanying cameraman, were jamming their respective equipment in the face of another neighbor, known as Snoopy Annette, who was taking her pug on his daily morning walkies. A second crew had gathered by our gate. They approached my car as I pulled out of the driveway.

"Do you socialize with Mr. Wells?"

"Does he entertain often?"

"Is he a good neighbor?"

One reporter forced a cameraman up to my window and began speaking into her microphone.

"Is your husband at home, Ms. Carbury?"

They knew my name?

"Is it true that your husband represents Clifford Wells?"

I inched by our front gate. Another cameraman had edged past my car and was heading for the house. Macduff and Abby sounded the alarm from inside as Nick opened the door.

Cliff appeared at the bottom of his driveway in his Land Rover.

The herd left me and stampeded west. As I rounded the bend, I caught a glimpse of the scene at my front door. The cameraman was limping at an impressive pace back toward the road. Nick waved goodbye to me. Good terriers.

Nick was home that night. I made reservations at The Grill, and we were seated promptly at seven. I ordered a Grey Goose martini with three olives. Nick made a face and requested Glenlivet on the rocks. I settled in to hear about his day.

"Cliff is naturally disturbed that the press has found him here. I always said that it was just a matter of time."

"Did they get anywhere with him this morning? I didn't stay to watch."

"He says that he just shook his head at them and kept going. But it won't stop there."

"Has there been any new information on the girl who was killed?"

"Supposedly the investigation continues."

"Does Cliff have any plans to return to England?"

"No. It would be worse over there."

"Nick," I began, spearing my endive salad, "I'm thinking of approaching the partners about making a shift in my practice. I want to drop the family nonsense—do some real civil trial work."

"Makes sense, as long as they pay you more." He laughed. "They could hardly pay you less."

"My decision is as much to do with job satisfaction as it is with money."

"I would prefer that you concentrate on the money. I'm tired of paying all the bills, and doing all the work. I make four times what you do. Time you started pulling your weight in this marriage." He finished his whiskey and signaled the waiter for another.

I was so stunned, I couldn't respond. We finished our meal in silence.

That night I had two dreams.

I'm in a bedroom with lots of unknown people, moving furniture out. The wall behind the dresser is light green, and there is a heart etched into the wall. Macduff and Abby start fighting, and we have to separate them.

In the second, a dead body, obviously female and wrapped like an Egyptian mummy, is lowered through the top of a skyscraper into a sarcophagus. The feeling is of stealth and secrecy. I pour oil over the corpse and chant something.

I researched these symbols on the internet. Bedrooms usually pertained to the unconscious, rather than sex or intimacy. Therefore, dreams that took place in the bedroom were signals of issues that had more of an impact on our lives than we realized, and needed to be addressed. Green was the color of healing. The heart was our emotional center—how we were dealing with our own feelings. Dogs tended to deal with loyalty, but I couldn't find any direct reference to canine disputes. Cats and dogs, on the other hand, represented the conflict of our female and male sides. Our female half was our emotions; the male was our logical or rational mind. Was Abby my female side in this scenario?

The mummy was more difficult. Was she a pun for "mommy"? But that analysis did not fit in with the other symbols. What about wrapping? According to one site, this meant that I had been hiding my true feelings. Another expert reported that bodies or corpses signified a major change in your life. In comparison, a dream involving suicide revealed a complete transformation, and a wish to leave the old life behind. But why was I singing over

my dead self, and why all the mystery? Ointment was about healing and soothing past pain. Singing could be spirituality or feelings. Buildings were symbols of ourselves. Was I a skyscraper?
A tower of strength? Burials and funerals dealt with the need
to bury the past, or in the alternative, were a clue about buried
feelings.

My Book Club met at the Westport Library to discuss *Persuasion*.
I thought about Anne Elliot's mean-spirited, self-centered sisters,
and realized that people really hadn't changed much in two hundred years.

"There have been many biographers of Austen," I reported.
"Unfortunately, very little is known about her. We have some of
her letters, and memoirs written by family members. Probably a
lot of glossing over and halo-waving went on there."

"Most historians tell us what we already know," Denise agreed.
"The writing is invariably choppy, and the authors appear to be
merely paraphrasing Austen's letters. I bought a documentary on
DVD about her last year, and was very disappointed. Most of the
information concerned Austen's brothers, the naval ones in particular, and the history of the time. Not much that was intimate."

Dottie introduced the topic of Austen's novels in general. Who
was the greatest hero of all her male characters?

"Knightley," Eliot said, promptly. "All the other men were either
weenies or rakes. Look at Edward Ferrars and Charles Bingley.
Consider Henry Crawford and George Wickham."

"I did *not* enjoy *Mansfield Park*," said Denise.

"Colonel Brandon was surely the epitome of the silently suffering soldier, and Mr. Darcy was hardly a weak personality," Jane
replied.

"Darcy was convinced of his own importance, certainly, and
was inclined to follow the same tired shibboleths that his parents

had before him," Dottie remarked. "That is, until Elizabeth let him have it when he proposed to her the first time."

"What was the boyfriend's name in *Northanger Abbey*?" Eliot demanded.

"Henry Tilney."

"Another weenie."

"We appear to have abandoned the intellectual aspects of this discussion," Jane said. "Let us return to Mr. Knightley. What were his attributes?"

"He tried to teach Emma some social graces. He had very high standards of proper behavior," said Eliot.

"He was controlling and interfering," Dottie replied.

"He was only jealous of Frank Churchill," Denise added.

"Another man with an agenda," I sighed.

"I find that Knightley and Darcy are very similar," Jane argued. "Arrogance, driven by selfishness, which often leads to foolish behavior, was then tempered in the end by an apology. And, of course, a wedding."

"Why didn't you like *Mansfield Park*, Denise?" I asked.

"Not a bit romantic! Poor Fanny. She was a consolation prize."

"The progression of an Austen plot is secondary to her brilliance with the language. One must discern the many layers of meaning in her dialogue to truly appreciate her work," Jane replied.

"What's your vote for Austen's best hero, Dorothy?" I asked.

"Captain Wentworth. He had no money or connections and was sent away. He came back eight years later with a fortune in navy plunder. He never forgot Anne. He never lost his focus."

"Yes. Anne allowed Lady Russell's opinion to sway her. Wentworth reappears in her life, bitterly resentful. He perceives Anne as weak. If Wentworth had returned from the sea, a poor man still, would their reunion have been the same?" Denise wondered.

"I think so," Dottie said. "She refused Charles Musgrove and was never attracted by her cousin, even before she knew of his duplicity. Anne and Wentworth remained firm in their devotion to each other. Austen enabled them to convey their feelings in two separate instances by being overheard as they were speaking to a third party."

"True," I replied. "Anne, while on the other side of the hedge, listened to Wentworth and Louisa; and later Wentworth, while he wrote that letter at the White Hart, audited the conversation between Anne and Harville. Both times, the discussion was about the constancy of affections between men and women."

"But don't forget that Wentworth tortured Anne by appearing to court Louisa Musgrove. He didn't renew his attentions to her immediately, you know," Denise said.

Jane flipped to the end of the novel. "It is after the episode at Lyme that Captain Wentworth begins to see the light regarding Anne as opposed to Louisa. Anne has been on the periphery of the group until this point in the story. Suddenly there is an emergency, and Anne is at its center. It's an impressive transformation; a formerly reticent woman becomes powerful. Consider the following passage: 'he had not understood the perfect excellence of the mind with which Louisa's could so ill bear a comparison; or the perfect, unrivalled hold it possessed over his own. There, he had learnt to distinguish between the steadiness of principle and the obstinacy of self-will, between the darings of heedlessness and the resolution of a collected mind.' Wentworth appreciates Anne as the more balanced of the two women. He knows that he has been a fool."

"Maybe so, but he still wanted her to suffer first!" Eliot scoffed. "Weenie!"

No, not much change at all in two hundred years.

I ran into Lisa in the tack room after my ride. I hung up my bridle, and she came over and sat on the trunk next to mine.

"Em, Jack and I have decided to turn our place into a horse farm, and we would like to offer Joy a stall," she paused, "that is, if you're interested."

"I'm definitely interested! You know I haven't been happy boarding at show barns. What is your time-table?"

"The architect is working on the plans for the new barn now. We can fix up the old barn for the time being. We also have men coming in to put in the ring, and the paddocks. May I get back to you in a few weeks?"

"Absolutely! Thanks so much Lisa!" I pulled off my half-chaps and paddock boots, and tied my sneakers. "I've felt so disconnected from Joy lately. Not having to listen to Nick complain about her show expenses every month will be a big help."

"I get plenty of that from Jack myself," Lisa said.

"Do you know what a mid-life crisis is?" I asked.

"I think Jack is having one now," she grinned. "He says that he's re-evaluating his existence, what he's accomplished, and what he wants to do from now on."

"What fun for you!"

"Oh, he'll be fine. Like many men, he defines success as the amount of expensive stuff that he has accumulated. Jack will never see that happiness is how you feel on the inside."

"Has he ever said how he feels on the inside?"

"Has any man? They have too much fear of what they'd see. It's so much safer to measure with tangible items."

"I read somewhere that happiness is doing something that one is afraid of, every day; that it is purely a matter of attaining personal goals. One of the dream books I bought says that happiness can only be found by living in the moment."

Lisa frowned. "I feel like it's those things, and then so much more. We're all very different, and we all have our own baggage to sort through and release. This is why I find the mental health profession so ridiculous. Patients are lumped into a specific category from the diagnosis bible, and handed a prescription. So many people are lost due to inattention from the very experts who are supposed to be helping them."

"I know. But the judges order evaluations, and what are we supposed to do? Until alternative therapies are taken seriously, the poor souls who really need assistance are helpless."

"Have you thought about taking up yoga? It's more than just stretching. The breathing techniques are supposed to be very beneficial to emotional balance."

"The psychic said the same thing. I've found some night classes at the Warwick Community Center. I'm enjoying it, and I admit that I feel more grounded and balanced as a result. I think even my riding is starting to improve."

"Good. You'll figure this out, Em. You're so smart, and I've never known you to fail at anything that you're really focused on."

"Thanks. I have a feeling that this is all about clearing out my childhood, and possibly my first marriage. I've finally admitted to myself that my present marriage is not in a good place, but where I'm to go with that, I haven't a clue. I promise that I won't give up until I know."

Kim sat down at the library conference table looking nervous. I felt the same way. In five minutes a new client, Rosalind Stewart, would be arriving. Her daughter, Samantha, had just admitted to the family's therapist that she had been molested by her father from the time she was seven years old. This would be my first divorce case involving incest.

"Let's review the facts before she gets here," I said, taking a deep breath. "Rosalind and Christopher have been married for nineteen years. They live in Greenwich, just north of the Parkway. There are three minor children issue of this marriage: Sam is the oldest, at 16. Adam is 14 and Andrew is 11. Rosalind claims that the marriage began to go sour after Sam was born, and had all but disintegrated by the time the boys came along. Rosalind says that a year or so after Andrew arrived, she was very much involved in her mother's last illness, and was rarely at home, taking the boys with her, and leaving Chris to care for Sam."

"And that's when the creep got to her," Kim snarled.

"Apparently. God, this is awful. Anyway, as I said, Samantha is now 16, and a high school junior. She's always been difficult—mood swings, violent outbursts, dramatic weight changes, lack of sleep due to nightmares, an underachiever at school. Her mother reports that Sam has never been able to keep a friend for long; she always finds a reason to back off from any kind of emotional intimacy. Sam had her first date this fall, to the Homecoming dance, and there was a huge blow up with the boy. It seems that he got a little fresh with her in the car. Sam became even more isolated after this altercation, and all of her behaviors were exacerbated. Finally, Rosalind took her to a psychiatrist who specializes in working with teenage girls. The therapist, who is very experienced with child sexual abuse cases, asked Sam if she had any sexual experience, and the poor girl lost it."

"So the therapist told the mother? Can she do that? I thought therapy was confidential."

"There's a statute in Connecticut that forces doctors, teachers, ministers et cetera to report known cases of child abuse. Rather than calling the police, the therapist called our client."

"So now there's a restraining order against the father?"

"Yes, but only as to the daughter. Remember, it's the child's word against the father's. He's an affluent corporate executive, and politically connected. He's not going to roll over and admit that he's a pedophile."

Annie ushered Rosalind Stewart into the conference room, took her coat and an order for a cup of decaf tea, and left quickly, carefully closing the door behind her. Rosalind draped her designer clad frame on to a chair next to Kim.

Rather than addressing the custody and visitation issues first, I decided to ask about the financial situation, trying to keep the atmosphere somewhat level. This attempt failed miserably.

"Did you see that the bastard asked for joint custody of all three children in his cross complaint, Emma?" Rosalind demanded. "And that there's a motion for visitation? The judge ordered him to stay away from Sam!"

"That's family law tactics, I'm afraid." I sighed. "Your husband's lawyers want to get you riled up so that it looks like you're the reason for the breakdown of the marriage. Every salvo they throw will be calculated to grind you down. They'll focus on the money, and custody, and they'll claim that you forced Sam to make these accusations against her father. It's a smoke screen."

"Well, it's working!" Rosalind barked, pulling a silver lighter out of her Hermès bag and lighting a cigarette. Kim slid an ash tray toward her and scooted away from the stream of smoke that had hit her in the face.

"You want to know something?" Rosalind continued, clearly out of control with rage. "My kid is blaming me for this! She says that if I'd been home, instead of off with Grandma, her dad never would have touched her. She's defending him for God's sake! Now she just locks herself in her room. She's a bigger problem than ever before! And the disgusting slime ball has her convinced that the incest is all my fault!" Rosalind started to sob. "He was taking her in the pool with him and having her sit on his erect penis, and she says that I should have been there to save her."

"I'm asking the judge for a court ordered psychiatric evaluation of Sam's condition. It's ridiculous to think that any young girl
would make up a story like that." I could hear my voice shaking.
Kim was trying not to cry. "We're going to nail the man to the
wall, don't worry. When you're feeling a little stronger, we will want
to discuss the possibility of bringing criminal charges against your
husband. But that's a decision for you and Samantha to make."

"She'll never do it," Rosalind replied. "She won't hear a word
against her father. She won't talk to me at all, only to the therapist. I feel as though I've lost my daughter. I can't believe this is
happening!"

"Do you know when the incest stopped?"

Rosalind sniffed. "Sam told the therapist, in front of me, that
the touching stopped right around the time that she got her first
period. She was twelve. Since then it's been comments about her
body, and what she's wearing. Sam says that her father kept asking
her if she was having sex with boys. It's why she never went out on
dates, although she's always been very flirtatious, especially around
older men."

Kim cringed.

"I'll get going on these motions, then, and I'll be back to you
shortly. In the meantime, I suggest that you have regular sessions
with Sam's therapist yourself. This is a colossal blow to your family.
Make sure that you take care of yourself."

That evening I was in my study painting, when I heard ferocious growling coming from the family room below. I peered over
the banister. Macduff and Abby, who normally behaved reasonably
well together, were locked in fierce combat over Abby's stuffed cow.
I yelled to Nick, who came running in with a bucket of ice water.

I met Laura for lunch in Westport. We were seated at a table with a view of the Saugatuck River.

"How's Steve?"

"He flew to Seattle this morning. He'll be back Sunday night."

"It's always nice to have a little break in the routine."

"You have no idea. It's like letting pressure out of a tire."

"Is something specific going on?"

"No. But I have a theory about marriage. My marriage, anyway. I am Steve's energy bank. He draws on me and draws on me until I have nothing left. A shapeless jelly; lying there. Quivering. Not that he would notice this. And then, mercifully, he has a business trip, and I can replenish my stores." She sighed. "I just wish he would give more and take less."

"It's enough to make you want to slap their mothers around. This stuff doesn't happen by accident."

"It *is* like raising a very large child. Steve makes a production of everything he does. No one else has life as difficult as he has it. He's a noisy person. Pounding footsteps up and down stairs. Doors and cabinets slammed. The television on too loud. When he is away, the silence is marvelous. I find myself sitting very still sometimes, just listening to it."

"It's why we ride, right? And why we garden and I paint. If we don't protect our sanity, no one else is going to do it for us."

"And you have the stepkids."

"They're out of town most of the time. It was a lot tougher when they were still in Warwick High and living at their mother's. Dropping in uninvited. Dropping in when they knew that we weren't home. Needing and wanting; expecting and demanding. They still have keys to both houses."

"What will happen when they have kids of their own? Lots more wanting and demanding."

"I know. Thankfully, Nick is even less fond of children than I am."

I stopped by the Warwick Market on my way home. I'd had a craving for basil all day and decided to pick up some mozzarella and tomatoes as well. I ran into Jane in the cheese section.

"How's school?" I asked her.

"I've been approached about the department chairperson's position, which opens up in the fall."

"How exciting! Are you going to accept?"

"I think so. They've promised that I will have less of a course load, and, of course, there's the money."

"Have you ever had an administrative job before?"

"No. That is my one misgiving about this opportunity. I have a tendency to say what I think."

"Well, just say it politely."

"I can retire in a few years, anyway. I've done my time with this school board." She brightened. "How are you doing with *Lies Across America*?"

"I am excessively diverted, as Miss Bennet would say. I can't *wait* to hear Eliot's views."

"Yes. Perhaps we can limit her to expressing only one or two."

CHAPTER SIX

Research Shock

I left the office a little early to get to the barn for my lesson.

Joy and I trotted and cantered over poles for a while. Then we trotted over a cross rail.

"She's pretty quiet today," remarked Jeannie. "This may be the day we start cantering to jumps."

Yes!

"We'll do the usual cross rail first. Just stay still and keep your eyes up."

I managed a lovely, collected canter on the left lead, and we zeroed in on our target. Something told me to grab mane. Good thing.

"WOW!" I heard Jeannie exclaim as we launched over the jump. I had my eyes glued to the opposite wall and didn't dare to look down.

"What?" I asked. Jeannie had turned slightly pale.

"Do you know how high you went?" Did I want to know?

"Big?"

"Huge!"

Clearly, grabbing mane is of the essence when one jumps with Joy.

"She's so much fun!" I was gleeful. "She does all the work and really pushes you into position."

I patted Joy's neck and stretched forward to scratch behind her ears. What a good girl!

"I'm really impressed with your progress. The two of you are going to make a wonderful team. I think we'll work on singles for a while," Jeannie added, "before we try getting you down a line."

That night, I dreamed that I'm back living at Audrey's in Ridgefield. Kate is in the bedroom down the hall, and Dad is still alive. The house is in the dilapidated shape of my high school years: peeling paint, cracked driveway, white fence falling down on itself. The living room is a clutter of old newspapers and magazines, and the kitchen counters are covered with pots and dishes that need to be washed. My room, always a tidy oasis in real life, is in my dream as squalid and depressing as the rest of the house. Dad is sprawled on the couch, drunk and disoriented, and Audrey is sitting next to me at the dining room table. "May I just have a tiny corner of your pie, dear?" And then the inevitable snarl: "You miserable wretch! After all I've done for you?" I can hear Kate blasting her stereo and shrieking along with Mick Jagger, and Bailey, our beagle, baying to get out the front door.

Annie popped her head in my office the next morning. "Your ghost client is here."

I had decided to take a practical tack.

"John, your ex-wife's lawyer has filed a motion for a court-ordered psychological evaluation. This is not a surprise. We can put an agreement on the record, which would save the cost of a hearing."

"Fine, fine."

"I thought that I would suggest a group in Westport that I've worked with before. They are a team of forensic psychiatrists. They will interview you both alone and with the children, and then issue a report."

"Will they come to my home?"

"No, they conduct the evaluations in their office."

"Will I be allowed to see the report?"

"Yes, of course."

"Patty is going to tell them that I'm a whacko, isn't she?"

"I can't predict what she will say. But since she is asking the court to modify the original visitation orders, I think it is safe to assume that she will not paint you in the most positive light."

"Well, I'll agree to the exam. What choice do I have?"

"Patty's lawyer has also filed a motion to have an attorney for the children appointed. Do you have any objection to that?"

"We didn't have one for the divorce."

"There was no need then. You agreed to everything fairly quickly."

"Patty always gets what she wants. She wanted the divorce and the kids, so I gave them to her. Now, she doesn't even want me to see them."

"We haven't lost yet. But please don't talk about your grandmother to anyone else. I'll let the other side know that we have no objection to their motions."

Kim had done some research on the Web, and had duly ordered several books on the subjects of incest and sexual abuse. She dropped the opened box on my desk with a grimace.

"Don't worry," I assured her, pulling them out one by one. "I'll go through these. Thanks for finding them."

"Sorry," she said. "But this is personal for me. My college roommate was a victim of incest—her older brother. He used to drag her down to the basement and molest her on an old sleeping bag.

He was in high school, she was ten. By the time I knew her, she was bulimic, and nearly died from it. I could never keep food in the fridge, because she would stuff it all in her mouth, and then go throw it up. She never finished school. I hear that she's still living with her mother, and on heavy medication."

"That's horrible! Couldn't her therapist help her?"

"No one believed her. They said she made the whole thing up about her brother. She was diagnosed as bipolar. The incest was never addressed. Her therapist didn't know what the hell he was doing." Kim looked sad. "At least Sam has a good one."

"Yes. Let's hope that she can get through to the judge."

I began to read.

The horrible truth about incest is that it is a common occurrence. Millions of people have suffered from depression, anxiety, mood swings, fear of abandonment, eating disorders, trouble with interpersonal relations, and addictive behaviors as a result of the damage caused by incest. Research shows that most incest perpetrators are fathers, and most victims are their young daughters. The experts claim that incest has become epidemic, and that it occurs at every socioeconomic level.

Whether the incest is physical, or emotional, the common factor is secrecy. The child is threatened with a variety of frightening losses: breaking up the family, fear of imprisonment of the predator, abandonment, physical harm to the child or someone she loves—even her pet. The great damage is the violation of the bond of trust between a child, and the adult whom he or she trusts. The child is dependant on her abuser, and therefore trapped. She feels unsafe in her own bed.

Incest does not necessarily involve touching. The experts label this form of abuse as "psychological," "seductive," or "covert" incest. Behaviors vary: showing the child pornography, masturbating in front of the child, speaking to the child about sex, voyeurism, or giving the child inappropriate gifts such as sexy underwear. The child may be elevated by the perpetrator to the role of spouse-confident. This abuse isolates the child from both parents, and robs the child of his or her childhood. Often the "Silent Partner," usually the child's mother, is blamed by the child for lack of protection and interest. The predator parent, however abusive, is held harmless.

Adult survivors of incest suffer from a variety of symptoms, which are often misdiagnosed as cases of borderline personality disorder, bipolar disorder, or schizophrenia. They have been labeled "crazy," when what they really are is traumatized. Therapy is available, and the experts claim that group therapy is most effective, as speaking in front of fellow survivors destroys the secrecy and shame which has kept the incest victim silent for so long.

Incest is about fear, humiliation, and obedience. It has been described as the worst kind of abuse that can happen to a child. It is time to take the taboo out of incest. Professionals must be trained to detect the indicators of a child victim. Therapists should be encouraged to form incest support groups. Medical doctors, police, teachers, ministry, judges, attorneys and prosecutors should all be educated in order to get these children the help that they desperately need. Above all, they must believe the children.

I checked my watch, it was nearly 6:30. The office was silent outside my door. I kicked off my shoes, sat on the carpet, and hugged my knees to my chest, breathing slowly.

I had scheduled a meeting with the partners the following morning to discuss my preference for taking civil litigation cases. Mr. McCook, Basil, David, and Ed met with me in the library.

Basil Noles started the meeting at nine-thirty. I sat between Ed and his father. David glowered at us from across the conference table.

"I've always felt that your brains, and your talent, were wasted on couples squabbling," Mr. McCook said, kindly. "On that note, Basil has some good news for you."

I sat back, surprised. I had come prepared for a battle of sorts, and found myself dumbfounded, as Basil pushed a big file toward me.

"We've agreed to have you begin second seating me on the big accident cases. I need help," he threw a disgusted look at David, who was doodling at the other end of the table, "and you're very experienced with deposing experts and dealing with defendant's counsel. Kim can pick up the slack with the easier divorces, and Ed can take over some of your other files. The transformation will have to be gradual, but it will happen. You will naturally be receiving a percentage of the cases that generate money; more if you bring the case into the office. Does that sound all right to you?"

"It sounds perfect. Thank you." Relief. This meant interesting work, and bigger cuts on the contingency wins. Finally, my career was moving in the right direction. More money equaled freedom. I could let go of the fear of losing my horse. And it would relieve the tension at home.

Part II Trial

A formal Judicial examination of evidence and determination of legal claims in an adversary proceeding.

Black's Law Dictionary

CHAPTER SEVEN

Applied Kinesiology

The Dartmouth hockey team was playing at home both nights that weekend, so Nick and I packed up the terriers and drove to New Hampshire. We had often arrived at the lake after an absence of a few weeks to find that the pipes had frozen and the electricity was out. That weekend we were in luck.

"Do you want to have dinner in Hanover before the game?" Nick asked.

Not exactly my idea of the perfect Valentine's Day evening.

"I suppose that a romantic, leisurely dinner at some ye old inn and not going to the game at all is out of the question?"

"Definitely. This is a big weekend. The Dartmouth team is ranked fourth in the ECAC."

"And where is my Valentine's card?"

"Damn! I left it in my desk drawer."

We proceeded to Murphy's in Hanover and ordered drinks and dinner at the same time. Nick repeatedly checked his watch. It would never do to miss the first face-off.

The Thompson arena parking lot was crammed with enthusiastic fans in green and white. We presented our season tickets, grabbed a program, and shoved our way over to the concession stand where Nick bought two hotdogs and a coffee.

"We just had dinner, Nick!"

"I know. But I'm hungry again."

All the lights were extinguished. A spot light was aimed at the ice. The Rensselaer Polytechnic Institute Engineers appeared in their red and white uniforms.

"AAAND NOWWWW, THE DARTMOUTH BIG GREEN!" the announcer roared. The school band fired up its drummer. The young men skated out and the first line was introduced. A female emerged to sing the national anthem.

I took out this month's copy of *The Watercolorist Magazine*.

"Aren't you even going to watch?" Nick was indignant.

"I can do both; trust me."

I was engrossed in an excellent article on the technique of lost and found edges in landscapes, when I noted some intense activity at the Dartmouth end of the ice.

"Penalty against Dartmouth; high sticking," said the announcer. A player down, the Dartmouth team reassembled in their defense box formation. RPI swooped in on their power play.

I noted some new combinations of grays that would be wonderful for shadows on snow.

The crowd moaned. I assumed that the RPI team had scored. I checked the board. Yep.

The RPI fans shrieked "YOU JUST SUCK!" at the Dartmouth goalie.

Nick was despondent. "I could see that coming," he reported. The buzzer went off to mark the end of the first period. The Zamboni rolled out to resurface the ice. I got up to get some hot chocolate.

Nick was scanning the program when I got back. "Four out of

the five guys on the first line are from Canada," he said. "They are all six-two or taller." Fascinating.

The second period had begun. Dartmouth got control of the puck. The whistle blew. Icing.

I pulled out this month's issue of *Victorian* magazine.

"There it is!" shouted Nick in my ear. The band played their rendition of *My Girl*. The score was tied.

"This line is all freshmen," Nick remarked. "The center is from New Haven."

RPI charged across the ice with the puck.

Oooo, a weekend of watercolor painting in Paris in May.

More moaning. The RPI fans screamed "YOU'RE A SIEVE!" at the Dartmouth goal tender. You had to admire their sportsmanship.

"Look, the coach is putting the second string goalie in."

I examined the recipe for brioche. It looked complicated.

"Penalty against RPI. Penalty against Dartmouth. Roughing." The guys were four-on-four on the ice.

"Penalty against Dartmouth. Cross checking." The Big Green was down to three against four.

"They can't lose any more players, right?"

Nick looked at me in disgust.

Mass hysteria from the populace. Dartmouth was in a breakaway.

Both teams piled up on the RPI goalie. The net fell over on him. Ouch.

"HEADS UP IN THE STANDS!" said Mr. Announcer. The puck sailed over the glass and narrowly missed a student in a moose-shaped hat.

I flipped to an article on wineries. Why would anyone want a job turning champagne bottles every day?

The buzzer sounded the end of the second period. The Zamboni backed out again. I watched the driver manipulate the huge vehicle around and around and around.

"We didn't know you both were coming up this weekend!" Pete and Jane were standing in the aisle, waving. "Happy Valentine's Day!" said Jane. We looked at each other.

"Good game, huh?" said Pete. I motioned for him to take my seat. He and Nick began to converse in Hockey Speak.

Jane and I walked up the steps and stood by the railing.

"Did you get a card, at least?" I asked.

"No, but I did get some pretty red carnations from the market." We contemplated the men.

"Amazing, aren't they? Nick could tell you team statistics from 1953, but he can't ever remember where I keep the scissors. The same kitchen drawer, by the way, that his first wife had them for almost twenty years."

The coaches walked back across the ice. Time for the third period.

"Would you both like to come back to our place for drinks?"

"Thanks, Jane. We'd love to."

Dartmouth lost, four to two. Nick took the left lane to merge onto Route 89 South.

"RPI got some real garbage goals tonight," he lamented.

"They still count the same, though."

"The goalie had no support. They really need to work on their defensive strategy."

I spent all of Sunday morning setting up the lake house for Nick's annual Men's Scratchfest, which was to be the following weekend. This entailed making up the eight spare beds, plus cleaning all three bathrooms and putting out towels. For years I had begged Nick to hire a cleaning crew, but he refused to spend the money. He waved off such menial details as my responsibility.

I found Nick in front of the television, watching the political pundits.

"You're all set for next weekend."

"Thanks." The Secretary of State was being interviewed.

"There are plenty of breakfast necessaries in the refrigerator, including juice, coffee, eggs, and bacon."

"Do we have marmalade?"

"Yes." Nick resumed his morning coma.

"When do you want to leave?" I asked.

"After lunch. I have a game tonight."

I had to be in court in Stamford on Monday morning for short calendar. Mrs. Bissell had recently declared that she was afraid of her husband of thirty-four years and wanted exclusive possession of the marital home. I represented Mr. Bissell. I met him on the third floor.

"OK Carl, tell me what you did with the guns."

"My brother has them in his closet."

"And the hunting knives?"

"I gave them to my son."

"What about the staple gun?"

"Oh, come *on*, Emma!"

"She's worried about the staple gun. Where is it?"

"In the basement."

"You need to find a new home for it, for the time being."

"This is ridiculous. Do you realize that she had a huge dead-bolt put on our bedroom door? I haven't touched the woman in years!"

"Emotions get a little out of control during a divorce. But you want to stay in your house, right?"

"Yes, of course I do. I paid the mortgage for thirty years, while she sat on her butt all day."

"She was raising your three children, Carl. Now, what about the cross-bow?"

Annie slapped the Hartford paper on my desk that afternoon. "Have you seen this?" she asked. "Front page!"

MURDERING BRIT LIVING IN WARWICK

Clifford Wells, who was acquitted of murder in the sensational London trial last fall, is now living in leafy Warwick, Connecticut. Wells, who was president of one of London's largest brokerage firms, was accused of brutally murdering his assistant, Christina Lyon, who was found dead in her office last summer. Mrs. Wells has since filed for divorce in England. Mr. Wells is currently employed on Wall Street.

"Don't these people understand the concept of defamation? He was found not guilty!"

"He's Nick's client, isn't he?"

"Yes, on the civil side. Nick's not going to like this."

Friday morning, I had two L.L. Bean boat bags and the cooler packed for Nick's All Male Scratchfest.

"Mac's food is in this one. So is his coat. Make sure you put it on him if it gets really cold."

"I'll remember."

"I put all the bread items in the green bag. Don't forget to turn up the heat in all the bedrooms, especially the one on the basement level."

"I know, Em."

"You *will* walk him, right? I don't want him marking the furniture."

"I said I would."

"All right. Have a good time." The car pulled out and proceeded north.

Abby and I contemplated each other with delight. I let out a huge breath. Freedom!

"What should we do tonight?" I asked her. "Cook some hand-made pasta, open up some merlot, and watch a chick flick?"

"Berf!" Abby wagged her square little tail vigorously.

I went up to my study and considered my latest drawing, which was propped up on my easel. It was of a frozen waterfall, from some photos I had taken in Quechee, Vermont the winter before.

Abby leaped up on my chaise and settled herself comfortably against the pillows. I started a movie and began to lay in the first wash for the sky.

We were well along into the second tear-jerker when the phone rang. Nick.

"It's nearly ten below here, Emma! The snow is now piled higher than the deck, and the pipes are frozen again. I'm waiting for the plumber now. At least the power is still on."

"Are any of the guys there yet?"

"No, most of them are meeting me for dinner in Hanover."

"There's some bottled water in the fridge for Mac. If nothing else, you can melt snow."

"OK, thanks. I'll keep you posted."

Nine men in my house without showers or flush toilets. I ran downstairs and made myself a martini.

The phone rang. Nick again.

"The plumber says that the pipes are freezing because the heat's not working where the water comes into the utility room from the main. I called the electrician. He's coming tomorrow morning."

"But you have water now?"

"Yes, but there's no guarantee that the pipes won't be frozen again in the morning. The forecast is for twenty-five below, tonight. I've left two space heaters going in there."

On Monday I stopped the car at our gate to get the mail. Clifford Wells pulled up in his Land Rover.

"Good evening, Emma."

"Nick says that he's been beating heads at the various newspapers."

"Yes. A few retractions so far."

"That must be very satisfying for you."

"Frankly, it just stirs up more attention. Do you know my neighbor to the right?"

"Snoopy Annette? Sure."

"Is that what you call her? Quite appropriate, really."

"Is she a bit too friendly? Just be blatantly rude to her. We all are."

"Thanks."

"I understand that you have a television interview coming up soon."

"I leave for Los Angeles tonight. When I get back, I'd love to have the two of you over for dinner."

"We'd be delighted. Are you going to cook?"

"Yes, indeed. I enjoy showing off my culinary talents."

"Great. We'll bring the wine."

I changed into old sweats and began sanding one of the patio side tables. It was painted iron and would need a coat of primer on the rusted areas. Mac stretched out on the bench and watched. I noticed that some of my shade perennials were beginning to make an appearance in the rock garden. A chipmunk emerged from the fieldstone wall, squeaked, and dived back in.

Suddenly I heard a soft plop, and then a chirp. I looked toward the screened porch and was startled to see a female cardinal hopping around on the glass table. How did she get onto the porch? My dilemma was getting her out through the door before Macduff was aware that we had company. I opened the door as quietly as I could, sliding the catch back to keep the opening as wide as possible. The bird leaped into the air, banged into the light fixture that was suspended from the ceiling, and hit the screen with a thud. She came to rest on a window ledge. Mac looked up.

I grabbed a chair cushion and got behind her, waving her toward the door. It took two trips, but the cardinal finally zoomed out onto the patio, shrieking in dismay. I checked all the screens for holes, but couldn't find any large enough for a bird to get through. Odd.

I resumed my project. Macduff lifted his head and sniffed the air. The temperature was still in the sixties, but I knew that the warm weather wouldn't last.

"We can have frost here until the middle of May," I said to Mac. I applied the white primer and left it to dry. "At least we can start some of the vegetables now." There wasn't much daylight left, but I quickly planted two rows of peas and three rows of lettuce in one of Nick's raised beds. Nick pulled up as I turned off the water.

"What did you want to do for your birthday?" he asked.

"It's a Monday this year."

"I know. I have a Ridgefield ZBA hearing that night."

"Can't you change it?"

"I tried. This matter was postponed from last month, and it's fairly urgent. Do you want to go out Sunday night instead?"

"Kate's making me a special dinner. She says that Hannah has something for me. Maybe I can get her to change it to Monday."

"Well, it's not for a couple of weeks yet. Let me know what you decide."

Dr. Rosie Travis was Laura's chiropractor. When I arrived for my first appointment with her the next morning, I found that Rosie was more than I expected.

"So you've never had an adjustment before?" she asked, rubbing her hands together like a mad scientist.

"No, but Laura says you're terrific, and I'm sick and tired of ...."

"Of feeling sick and tired?"

"Yes! I was looking at your brochure in the waiting room. You do acupuncture, nutrition, and allergy elimination as well?"

"I'm certified in many different holistic treatments, and they can all be geared to your specific needs. These treatments will guide you to internal balance and overall body well-being."

"What is Applied Kinesiology?"

"Muscle testing and treatment. The theory is that organ dysfunction can be distinguished by a specific muscle weakness. By testing different points on your body, I can determine what needs to be adjusted, or cleared. I can see that your jaw is out of alignment, just by watching you speak." She gently touched both sides of my face. Then she put on a latex glove. "Do you realize that the chewing muscles are the most powerful that we have? I'm going to 'milk' your muscles from inside your mouth. The right side is worse than the left. This may hurt."

It did, but I didn't protest and instantly felt better when Rosie pulled off her glove a few minutes later. "You're really grinding, especially on the right. You should consider going to your dentist for a night guard," she said, "before you do some real damage to your teeth."

"I've already had two crowns and a root canal in the last six months."

"I'm sorry, but I'm not surprised. Let's see what's going on with the rest of you."

I lay on my stomach with my face in the doughnut, glad about my decision to wear loose sweats and a T-shirt for this appointment.

"I'll adjust your pelvis in a moment," Rosie informed me. "The rhomboid under your right shoulder blade is very tight. I'll loosen that up first. Have you had any falls recently?"

"Just from my horse. Nothing unusual."

"There's a lock up here that must make it difficult to turn to the right when you're riding." She pushed down, and I heard a crack. "It should be a lot easier for you now. Let's check your neck."

I flipped over on my back. Rosie sat behind my head and gently touched the area just below my skull. "Your Atlas bone is doing something really funky," she reported. "Your neck is almost inverted. I'm going to adjust you on both sides. Please stay relaxed and go with it."

Laura had warned me about this maneuver. I closed my eyes and slowed my breathing. Rosie rotated my head so that my right ear was practically on my shoulder and gave a quick twist. I heard a crack. Then she repeated the same treatment on my left side. "Were you hearing a buzzing before?" Rosie asked. "I bet the nerves running through there were good and compressed."

"I was! I assumed it was a headache or a sinus infection."

"No," she smiled. "It was nerve damage. But don't worry, it's temporary."

We spent another half hour muscle testing and adjusting.

"Basically, you're hunched from stress, like a cat when it's feeling under attack. Your collar bones are pushed up, and your back muscles are sore from the strain. Try stretching in doorways to open up your chest muscles and give some relief to your back. You're protecting your heart." Her voice softened. "Stress is what makes us sick, you know. The body is set up to heal itself, but it needs support."

"Thanks. I'll remember that."

"Keep up your yoga. It's wonderful for opening up the energy pathways. Sleep with just one pillow. And remember to work on your breathing."

CHAPTER EIGHT

Conspiracy

Cliff provided us with drinks and then suggested the grand tour.

"This is the library. I just had it done over in navy and primrose. Most of the books and furniture I brought over with me from London. Here in the dining room is the mural that I was telling you about. It's a battle scene from the War of 1812 and was commissioned by the prior owners. I felt that it fit with the Federal style of the house and decided to keep it. The conservatory, which is more contemporary, is through here. I'm not thrilled with the wicker, but again, it fits."

"I love the antique plant stands," I said, admiring the gardenias. Marvelous aroma.

"I found those in Manhattan. Here's my study. Traditional English, wouldn't you agree?"

"But with much more individuality! Did you bring that screen over as well?"

"Yes. But I bought the cabinets in Boston and the rugs here in Connecticut."

"Who is the woman in the portrait?" Nick asked.

"My great grandmother on my father's side. She was the daughter of an earl and quite a character. Lady Emma." He grinned at me.

"Please tell us about her," I said.

"She was born around the turn of the previous century and lived an extremely privileged life until the war. Everything changed after that."

"How did she meet your great grandfather?"

"The usual story. She nursed him after he was injured and went back to Kent with him when he was fit enough to work."

"Is her father's estate still in your family?"

"Yes. It's in Devon; close to the sea."

We moved to the living room. A small woman in an apron was just setting out appetizers.

"I have recently acquired a Cajun cookbook. You both are my guinea pigs tonight."

Nick examined the assortment.

"Those items on the left are known as hot oyster puffets."

"And this dip?" I asked, grabbing a cocktail shrimp.

"Crab and artichoke. Better try a bit with a spoon first."

I was feeling pretty mellow after two glasses of Cliff's Meursault.

"So, Cliff. This family estate of yours. Are there any ghosts?"

"Actually there are. Why do you ask?"

"Emma has a client with other-worldly issues."

"Let's just say that I'm open to new concepts. I want to hear about your ghosts."

"They are reportedly those of ancestors who didn't care to relocate after they departed this life. They tend to appear most when a current family member is particularly unhappy or in trouble. They are benevolent rather than frightening."

"Have you ever seen one yourself?"

"As a child, many times."

"I never have," Nick said. "But I'm willing to accept that it could happen."

"How did you know?" I asked.

"That they were ghosts? They moved very fast. They didn't speak but managed to communicate, nevertheless. They just seemed to be aware of what was going on."

The small female reappeared. "Dinner is served."

I was seated with an excellent view of our house from the south window. The tuna with Cajun spices was perfectly cooked.

"Do you have any plans for your garden, Cliff?"

"I do indeed. I have hired a landscape architect to help me with a formal English garden. There will be paths and some sort of permanent structure. Perhaps a fountain."

"You're aware that we're in Zone Six, right? Don't expect English plants to survive our winters."

"Not to worry. This gentleman is quite good. I am anxious to start the project." There was a pause. "I read about your victory in the Connecticut Supreme Court last month, Emma. Congratulations."

"Thanks. I felt that I deserved to win the appeal since the trial was such an appalling disaster."

"The facts were certainly interesting. Former prostitute wanted custody of her niece and nephew after her sister committed suicide?"

"We never did prove the prostitute part. She definitely stripped and posed, however."

"The article said that she began threatening her brother-in-law with legal action before her sister was even buried."

"True. The trial judge found that the aunt showed the proper familial spirit."

The month of March passed mercifully out of our lives, and by early April we were finally able to recognize the signs of spring.

Denise called from her office in Hartford. "I saw your ex-husband in court this morning. He was there on a motion for summary judgment."

"Was it a good argument?"

"No. But he stopped to say hello to me and mentioned you."

"How'd he look?"

"Like he'd been hitting the meatball grinders again. The charm is wearing a little thin, though."

Shawn Patrick Timothy Kilcullen. Married him in my twenty-sixth year. Divorced him in my twenty-ninth year. Still embarrassed that I ever agreed to that second date.

"The Irish twinkle not working so well these days?"

"Maybe I just know too much about him."

"Running through three wives in forty years is not an impressive statistic."

The Book Club assembled at Eliot's townhouse in Darien to discuss the relationship between Virginia Woolf and her sister Vanessa Bell, in *A Very Close Conspiracy*, by Jane Dunn.

"I think we should start with the early years, when the Stephen children were growing up with their parents in London," Dottie said.

"I was astonished to discover that Virginia never went to college," Denise exclaimed.

"Yes, but go back further. Think about the dynamics of this household. Four half-siblings from the prior marriages of the parents, both widowed. Sir Leslie's daughter Laura was eventually labeled a lunatic and removed. Sir Leslie and Julia marry. Vanessa was born, followed by Thoby, Virginia and Adrian."

"The two girls were sexually abused by their half-brothers," Eliot contributed.

"They were both victims of incest. Their mother died. Their half-sister Stella got married and died. Then, Sir Leslie's long illness and death. Thoby's early death. Fast forward to Vanessa and Virginia as women; the unconventional marriages, the interchangeable relationships with the Bloomsbury group. Vanessa's affairs. Virginia's bouts of insanity from bipolar disorder."

"Don't forget her sojourn into lesbianism," Denise added.

"And underlying everything, the competitiveness between the sisters. Consider that Vanessa became their mother and Virginia their father."

"Wow," Eliot said.

"Let's break all that down," Jane said.

"Classic Victorian drama," I remarked. "Those people just loved a good death."

Dottie looked annoyed.

"Sorry, Dorothy. You're right. We have a lot of issues to examine. Art versus intellect. Fertility versus celibacy."

"I grant you the period gloom," she admitted. "The Stephen home was apparently classic: black paint, heavy drapes, massive furniture, stuffy. It's not surprising that these children developed into adults who were determined to be unfettered by convention."

"Let's explore one of your themes, then," Jane said. "The most obvious is the role of Woman to create order out of chaos for the people in her family. If you have read *To the Lighthouse*, you understand that this novel was Virginia's portrait of her parents. Julia stretched herself too thin and died. Stella took over, and died two years later. Vanessa became the earth mother."

"But she survived into her eighties. Interesting," Eliot said.

"Arguably, Vanessa became Virginia's mother as well," Denise said. "Vanessa was obviously a woman of very tough fiber."

"All right. It's 1904. Edward VII is on the throne. Sir Leslie Stephen finally makes his exit, to the relief of most of his offspring. What happens? How is Bloomsbury born?" Jane asked.

"The Stephens moved from Kensington to Bloomsbury. Life in the new century began with personal freedom. Thoby brought his Cambridge friends to visit; this progressed to open invitations every Thursday night, and thus the group evolved." I flipped to an early photograph of Vanessa painting.

"You look like her, Em," Eliot noted over my shoulder.

"Thanks. She died on my birthday." Everyone stared at me. "But not the same year."

"Vanessa had a passion for decoration and color," Denise said. "She was sensible and unsentimental. Virginia was a writer after generations of Stephens. She was shattered by her father's death, had numerous breakdowns throughout her life, and eventually drowned herself at the age of fifty-nine."

"They both had a series of sexual relationships that were less than orthodox. Virginia was involved in a very serious flirtation with Vanessa's husband Clive early in the marriage." Dottie turned to a picture of Vita Sackville-West.

"Vanessa had three children. Virginia never became a mother," Eliot said.

"Their work," prompted Jane. "Vanessa used her farm house as her largest canvas. Dunn writes that Vanessa created Charleston to be an ideal haven for the Bloomsbury crowd. Vanessa was able to harmonize domesticity with her art, and it was this balance which kept her sane. But what about Virginia? She didn't have the distraction of raising children to contend with."

"No, but she had her health issues. In the face of Vanessa's many successes, Virginia, for all her genius, must have felt completely inadequate," Dottie said.

"What? For not having a baby?" Eliot scoffed.

"For not being Vanessa. The fertility goddess. The Real Woman, if you will. Vanessa managed it all."

"So what was the Conspiracy between the sisters?" Jane asked.

Dottie considered the question. "Love and jealousy?"

"Survival of their childhood?" Denise suggested.

"Each one wanted to be the other?" Eliot proposed.

"I think that their lives were so deeply intertwined that it would be impossible to consider one sister without taking into account the other," I mused.

"Excellent, ladies. What should our selection be for next time?"

"Let's have a little fun. How about a mystery?" Dottie grinned.

"My all-time favorite is *Gaudy Night*. No mangled corpse, but several juicy themes to develop," Denise said.

"We'll meet at my house. It should be warm enough to use the porch by then," I added.

"Perfect. Ms. Sayers in Warwick, it shall be."

That night I dreamed that I am frantically trying to get to the airport. I am on a major highway somewhere in New York, with ramps everywhere, going higher and higher. There's a sensation of running out of time and unnecessary delay.

Then, I'm at the airport. I'm rushing to the gate, waving my boarding pass. An airline official is very frustrated with another woman who keeps moving in the wrong direction. The implication is that I make it to my plane, but just barely. I am concerned that my luggage isn't loaded on time.

Finally, there is a crocodile pond in the middle of my living room. The water is very clear. The crocodile leaps out of the tank and gets in my face.

An airport may indicate a big change in one's life. Was I the woman moving in the wrong direction? What was I missing? The psychic said that I did everything too fast. I should skate through life; take things as they come. How did we know when to act and when to sit still? Maybe that was the big secret.

Crocodiles symbolized troubles that lurked beneath the surface and struck very powerfully and very fast. I had no idea what this meant. Obviously I was being prepared for something, but from which general direction was not clear at all. Or was the croc representative of my energy? My ability to face issues with strength and speed?

Annie appeared at the door.

"Your mother's on the phone. She wants you to do a new will for her, but she doesn't want you to be the executrix."

"Beg your pardon?"

"Do you want to talk to her?"

"Good morning, dear."

"Yes, Mother."

"Did your girl tell you why I'm calling, dear?"

"Yes, my girl did."

"Well, dear. Your uncle was named executor of our wills years ago. But now that your father is dead and your uncle is in Maryland...."

"He's always been in Maryland, Mother."

"I thought it would be a good idea to do a new will. You *can* do wills, can't you, dear?"

"Yes, Mother. Who do you want as executor?"

"Well, I thought perhaps your sister Kate. She's *so* good with money."

"Let's see if I've gotten the gist of your request. You want me to draft a new will for you—free of charge, I suppose?"

"Naturally, dear."

"But you prefer that your other daughter, who is not licensed to practice law in this or any other state, be named executrix. Is that correct?"

"Yes, dear. How bright you are."

"I have to go now, Mother. I have an important lunch date."

"We can discuss this on Easter Sunday, Emma, dear."

"Looking forward."

The phone rang again. Kate. Laughing merrily.

"You have to admit it, the woman has nerve!"

"Yeah, she got me this time. Do you even *want* to be executrix?"

"I can barely spell it. No, of course not. But let her play with this for a while. Think of the mirth value."

"Fine, but remember that Nick's kids will be with us on Sunday, so I'm rather low on mirth at the moment."

CHAPTER NINE

Flat Tire

The night after Easter, I dreamed that Joy's old trainer, Hal, climbs into my car, sits on the dashboard and laughs at me because I've turned off my cell phone. I push the power button, and it rings. The tune is Ode to Joy. I answer, and Lisa tells me don't worry, Joy is fine, but that she needs a rest.

Then I'm at a dude ranch. My cell phone is turned off again. I have high heels on and clogs in the car. No boots or sneakers. Someone tells me that my cowboy boots are another year off. Then I yell at one of the barn employees: "I don't work for you—you work for me."

Third, I go to get into what is supposedly my Jeep. The door is open, and the inside is full of water. As I take off, someone yells something about my gear box. The emergency brake is hard in the up position and useless. Driving on the road is a nightmare. I have no gears or brakes, and I'm zooming up and down hills; dodging obstacles like big oil cans in the road. I come down a hill into a town and drive straight into a canal. I look to two policemen standing nearby to help me, but they're too busy gossiping to even notice me. So I pick up the Jeep and throw it back onto the road.

Nick and I were in our double shower the next morning. He handed me the soap, and instead of taking it, I moved forward and wrapped my wet arms around him. "We've never tried it in here," I murmured in his ear.

"I have to get going Emma," he replied brusquely, pushing me off. "The partners are meeting in an hour."

I stood there, dripping, while he opened the door and grabbed a towel. Ten minutes later I heard his car go up the driveway.

Annie met me at my office door with a huge ice coffee.

"You're wonderful," I said gratefully. "What's the occasion?"

"Thanks for the Secretaries' Day arrangement. I love peonies. You have some flowers as well."

"*I* do?"

"From the firm. The card says Happy Lawyers' Day." Annie scowled. "Ed brought them in about ten minutes ago. Kim got some too."

We each smirked appropriately.

"Also, I forgot to tell you that your ghost client was coming in this morning."

"That's OK. I don't have court today."

"There's more. He wants to do a séance at his house. With a medium."

"Aha."

"And he wants you to be there."

Who says the practice of law is a dull business?

"Look, John, I know you're upset about the psych eval, but this is a bit extreme. Are you expecting that your ex-wife will want to show up for this event? With her lawyer?"

"No harm in asking. The damage has been done. The judge is going to think I'm a total nut case when he reads that report."

"I have a question. If you can see your grandmother, why can't Patty?"

"The kids say it's because Patty isn't open to it."

"So how will a séance help? I can't pretend to know much about this stuff."

"A real professional medium will act as a conduit. It's hard to explain. Will you come?"

"Just let me know when. I can't wait to tell Ed about this."

"What will he care, as long as I pay my bill?"

A valid point.

Annie buzzed. "Warwick Bicycles called. Your mountain bike is ready to be picked up."

"Oh, good. Thanks." Now that spring was finally here, I could resume my evening rides.

I had a voice mail message from Lisa:

"Hi Em, I wanted to let you know. We've signed the agreement with the builder. The new barn is going up as soon as we get approval from the town. They've already started excavating for the ring. If the weather cooperates, it will be finished in a few days. The old barn should be ready by the end of next week. The paddocks are already done. We still have to find a trainer, though. Sharon has two more years left in the juniors, and she'd really like to qualify. Would you please give me a call?"

Clifford was pulling the mail from his box, when I stopped at our gate.

"How is your new garden coming along? I see trucks coming in and out of your place all the time."

"I've had the crew begin some of the beds and have ordered an assortment of benches and arbors. Unfortunately, the town officials are creating a bit of a bother about my proposed fountain."

"Why?"

"They say that the site is wetlands. I'm going to have to appear in front of the Inland Wetlands people."

"I've heard that the powers that be on Main Street simply adore toying with celebrities. Have you spoken to Nick about this? He was Warwick town counsel years ago. He's familiar with all the officials."

"I didn't know that, thanks. I'll call him directly."

I met Laura for lunch in Westport the next day.

"I've asked around about trainers, Em," she said. "There was a woman who rode for Madeline on a per diem basis. Olivia Thompson. She is supposedly quite competent with the big jumpers. And she isn't attached to a particular barn; she travels around."

"Did you know her?"

"Only to say hello. She grew up around here, but has spent most of her professional life in Massachusetts. She's only been back for a few months. Seemed pleasant enough."

"I'll give her a call, then. It's a start. Thanks, Laura."

"Any time. I think you're smart to rid yourself of the whole show barn scene. You're dealing with nothing but pure ego with those A Circuit people. They're so controlling. Once you move Joy to Lisa's, you'll be able to call your own shots."

"You're right. I'm ridiculously excited about grooming and bathing her myself. I want to learn to wrap her legs properly and clip her, and put her on a lunge line. I'll have direct contact with her farrier, her vet, and her dentist; no more barn manager playing middleman. Right now, I just ride and provide treats. I want the whole experience. It's why I got a horse in the first place."

"Besides," Laura grinned, "doesn't Joy get along with women better anyway?"

I turned out onto the Post Road heading west and felt a shudder and then a thump, thump on the right side of my Audi. There was a definite list. Flat tire. Damn! I pulled into the nearest parking lot and called Audi Roadside Assistance. "Have you stopped your vehicle in a safe location?" the woman asked.

An hour and a half later, I was back on Route 33, the spare in place, heading north toward Warwick. The rip was a sidewall tear, which meant replacing the tire, probably two, to maintain balance on both sides.

Lisa had left a message on my cell voice mail. *"The ring is almost done, Emma. They're spreading the footing next week, and the fencing around the ring should be done on Friday. I'm just waiting for the stall doors to be delivered, and then we'll be able to have horses on the property. Hopefully, by next Sunday. Have you heard from Olivia yet?"*

Abby and I went for a bike ride that afternoon. Nick had given me an L.L. Bean backpack for Christmas——the old-fashioned style that loads from the top. I checked the tires on my Trek, hoisted the terrier, and headed south on Stone Meadow Road. Abby twisted so she could face forward over my shoulder, her black nose sniffing the breeze. It was a gorgeous day. We rode by the tree farm and up past the reservoir. Miles of fieldstone walls. Once over the bridge, I stopped and got out my travel painting kit and a bottle of water. I tied Abby's leash to a tree and did a few watercolor sketches of the lake, with the waterfall in the foreground and the last of the dogwoods in bloom. Spring colors, unlike fall, are very difficult to reproduce on paper. They inevitably look either washed out or gaudy.

At four-thirty there was still plenty of warm sun. I stowed Abs and took a different route back, passing a group of road bikers on the other side. What a determined bunch they were, looking quite earnest with their neon colors and coordinated footwear. They appeared to be amused by Abby's furry little face popping out of the green pack, triangular ears flapping as we went by. Employees at the local nursery were unloading stacks of pine bark mulch with a forklift. Abby barked at the men working, and they turned and grinned at us.

It felt so good to have more daylight again.

I was in the back door, just as the house phone rang.

"Hi, this is Olivia. I'm very interested in talking to you about your mare!"

"Oh good! As I said in my message, I'm going to be moving Joy to my friend's private barn shortly, and we both need a trainer who would be willing to make barn calls."

"So, basically, Joy has done a lot of showing, but is still pretty green?"

"Right. Her previous trainers took short cuts; rushed her to jumps and got ribbons, but weren't much interested in getting her in a regular, flat work program."

"She's only just turned seven, though, so you haven't lost much time."

"No. But I've decided to change the emphasis drastically. I bought her to please myself, after all."

"What about your friend Lisa? How many horses does she have?"

"Two, and more boarders may be coming. It's invitation only."

"Very wise. Well, let's see; how about I meet all of you in Weston? That way I can see the facility and find out where your horses are in their training."

I went online to do a little research on séances. There are a lot of haunted people out there, apparently. One website had over a thousand requests for some kind of professional intervention.

There were hundreds of pictures of glowing orbs, filmy figures, and spooky cemeteries. Even if a large percentage of these stories were fabricated, it was still a formidable list of ghosts for just the tri-state area. I decided to go to the Warwick public library on Monday.

CHAPTER TEN

Hair Cut

Annie brought me my mail. There was a small ivory envelope addressed in tiny cramped script. Audrey.

> Emma dear,
>   I am enclosing a newspaper ad from White Flower Farm. They are having a marvelous sale on hybrid roses this month. Do please consider one or two for me on Mother's Day.
>   Love,
>   Mother

"Subtle, isn't she?" Annie said, reading over my shoulder.

"Like Lady Macbeth with a perm."

I stopped at the Westport liquor store for more Grey Goose vodka. I also picked up a bottle of dry vermouth, just in case.

I jumped back into my Audi, put it into reverse, and roared into a turn. There was a sickening thud. I got out for an inspection and found that I had rammed into a guard rail near the edge of the parking lot. There was a large dent in the bumper and some chipped paint. I got out my BlackBerry and called the dealership for an appointment. What was happening to my poor red car?

I had a lunchtime appointment to get my roots done the next day. Roberta, my stylist, mixed up my color and began to paint it on. I noted her reflection over mine. "New do, Roberta?"

"It is. I was getting bored with the big hair look." She was now sporting a head of burgundy and gold spikes. "Were you happy with your color from last time?"

"Definitely."

"It looks good, I think. The brown is nice and rich, and very shiny."

Roberta was fussing with layers of my hair in the back of my head. I could see her frowning in the mirror.

"But?" I asked.

"Have you been doing more riding lately? Wearing a lot of pony tails? There's some pretty serious breakage here. Look." She pulled a hand mirror from a drawer and held it up. I could see the damage. There was nothing more than a fringe of hair on the right side.

"Oh my God!" I shrieked, frightening two other clients.

"Maybe it's your water?"

"I don't know. What should we do?" I was practically in tears.

"It's going to have to be evened up all around. You can't leave it like this."

Damn that psychic!

I fumed in my chair the whole time Roberta was cutting, but after she had blown me dry with a big round brush, I had to admit to being thrilled with the result. The length was just short of my shoulders, and Roberta had given me a little up-flip.

"I love it!"

"Very fresh looking," Roberta agreed. "Want some sparkle dust?"

"Sure. Apparently I'm going for a whole new me."

I was walking Mac that afternoon when Clifford Wells pulled up in his Mercedes and stuck his head out of the window. I noted a very attractive blond woman in the passenger seat.

"Emma, hello. This is Camille." The vision smiled. "Camille and I would love to have you and Nick join us for dinner at the club this weekend."

"We'd be delighted. I'm not sure what Nick's schedule is. May I call you this evening?"

"Please do."

"It's a pleasure meeting you, Camille."

"I hope we'll see you this weekend. Cliff says such wonderful things about you both." We glowed appreciatively at each other.

That night I dreamed that there are hundreds of bouquets of roses on my front lawn, all in different pinks and creams.

Then, I'm in an antebellum house. The house is huge and venerable and a trifle shabby, but for some reason loaded with fabulous patchwork quilts. I'm wearing a hoop skirt and holding a candle that turns into a very full cup of tea. I spill a little on my dress, but there is no stain. The dress is almost a tea color, like old silk; also a little shabby, but still beautiful. The homeowner is a young woman in black. She jumps off the huge staircase and commits suicide.

Roses were the symbol of love and femininity, and pink was the color of love. I would like to think that this was who I really was inside; but, because I'd spent most of my life just trying to survive, I'd been crusted over with some kind of protective shellac. The patchwork quilts represented the combined experiences that made up our lives. I realized that this outer layer was dissolving, and it terrified me. What would I do without it?

The house was supposed to be me, but what was the pre-Civil War significance? Women were property? They had no rights? Candles could be enlightenment, wisdom, or spirituality. The cup was another feminine symbol, but I couldn't find tea in any of the books. The color black had to do with willingness to explore the unconscious. Suicide was symbolic of powerful transformation.

I scrubbed the garden grime from under my fingernails at two-thirty and called Olivia on her cell. She agreed to meet me in Weston at four. I took a shower, tossed Abby into the car, and proceeded on Cedar Road toward Weston center. Lisa's farm was up on a hill overlooking the reservoir. She and her husband had built a seven-thousand-square-foot home at the very top of the ridge. Six paddocks had been fenced off since my last visit, and the freshly completed ring was on the right as one drove up toward the house. Lisa was standing in front of the old barn, waving. Abby stuck her head out of the window and started to bark. Mimi, the tiger kitten, took off behind the enormous pile of topsoil that had been scooped up from the site of the new barn. Olivia's Chevy dually pulled up right behind me.

Olivia was a five-foot-six brunette with sparkling blue eyes and a big, cheery smile. Like most professional riders I'd known, there was a hint of arrogance mixed with the friendliness. Trial lawyers had similar demeanors, as did actors and surgeons. Performance and spotlight was a tough combination.

Lisa took us on a tour of the old barn. It was set up with six stalls, a feed room and a tack room.

"It's not pretty," she said, "but it will be functional until the new barn is up." We looked at the lovely old wood stalls and beams. "Just so you know, Sally and Betsy have both approached me about moving here, too. That will make five horses, plus Betsy's daughter's pony Ginger. I'm not sure if that will be too much for your schedule, Olivia."

"I'll work it out," Olivia grinned. "If the adults can ride in the mornings, it frees me up for the school kids in the afternoons. I will have shows on the weekends, you understand."

"That will be perfect," Lisa said. "If Sharon is showing, then I can stay home and hack with whoever is here."

"Exactly," I agreed. I was looking forward to more time alone with Joy, without a trainer hovering over us, every minute.

"When do you plan to move your horses, Lisa?" Olivia asked.

"On Saturday. Jack will be home, so he can help with the trunks and drive the trailer. We'll be making three trips. We'll do our two first, then Joy and the pony, then Sally and Betsy's horses."

"Okay," said Olivia. "Let me know when you're ready."

I decided to take the scenic route home from Lisa's. I opened the sun roof, turned up the volume on the *Mamma Mia!* CD, and was thundering around the reservoir, belting out the words to the title song, when I felt the now familiar shudder and thump, and then the inevitable list. I pulled over by the rail and got out. The right rear tire this time. What the hell was going on?

Two hours later, I was back in my study, looking up symbols. Tires had to do with confidence or self esteem; the image was of one being carried along regardless of the condition of the road or the weather. Great, but the punctures were real, and expensive! Why was this happening to me?

Clifford's beach club was situated on a spit of land in Westport, with splendid views of the Long Island Sound on three sides of the long, white building. We left my Audi with the parking attendant and were greeted in the foyer by a gentleman in a tuxedo.

"We are guests of Mr. Wells," Nick said. We were immediately led to a table on the south side of the dining room, directly in front of the great glass wall that separated us from the veranda and, beyond it, the Long Island Sound.

"It is still too chilly to serve dinner outside, but it's a nice evening to dine by the water." The gentleman smiled at me and floated away.

It was, indeed.

Clifford and Camille were shown to their seats five minutes later. I considered what an interesting contrast we made as women—she in her elegant black sheath and blond halo, and I in my elegant aubergine sheath (albeit three sizes larger) and mahogany mane. A friend had once described me as "athletic pretty." I had taken his observation as a compliment and still regarded it as such. But Camille's fragility was unnerving. How could anything so delicate survive in this world?

I gave myself a little shake and ordered a whisky sour on the rocks.

The men, predictably, began an intense discussion of sports, analyzing first the attributes of American football as opposed to rugby, and subsequently moving on to baseball versus cricket. I relished the sunset over the Sound and sampled my second cocktail. Camille was immobile, a serene expression on her face. Was she bored, enraptured, or merely a little drunk? How wonderful it must be to command such poise.

Clifford suddenly remembered his manners.

"Camille owns an art gallery in Soho, Emma. I've been telling her about your watercolors."

Help! "I just paint for fun," I replied quickly. "It's my retreat from listening to people's problems all day. I certainly don't pretend to be any good at it."

"Her teacher says she should consider selling some of her paintings," Nick announced.

"Well, they *might* have a market locally, but that's all." Was there a closet nearby that I could dive into?

"Many amateurs don't realize how talented they are. And then again, many professionals think too much of their own work. It's interesting." Camille smiled graciously at me. Marvelous composure.

"Camille and I are flying over to London tomorrow," Cliff said. "I would like her to meet my boys and see the country estate in Devon."

"How is your family doing?" Nick asked.

"The press has had other fish to fry, thank goodness, so we've had a bit of a breather lately. My brother and his wife have been very supportive. My boys live with their mother near Regent's Park. I have come to an understanding with Daphne, at least. I will have free access to them while we are in London. Daphne and I are selling the house in Bath," he said to Nick. "The proceeds will go into escrow until the divorce is final. That's part of the reason for this trip."

"You want to claim your personal items?" I asked.

"Exactly."

I glanced at Camille. "I'm looking forward to this, actually," she said. "Cliff says that there are some wonderful paintings and antiques."

"It sounds as if you're going to have a very full itinerary," I replied. "Are you familiar with London and the west country?"

"With London galleries, certainly. I've never been much for the outdoors, however."

Our entrees arrived. I had ordered fettuccine with mussels, garlic tomatoes and chunks of chorizo sausage. Nick had chosen rack of lamb. Cliff had requested Beef Bourguignon.

Camille nibbled on her endive with pear halves and goat cheese salad.

There was a message light blinking when we got home.

"Hhhhi Daaad, this is Deborah. Just wanted to let you know that I'm up here at the New Hampshire house with some friends. Everything's fine. Bye."

I could feel my face freeze in anger. "Did you tell your daughter that she could be at the lake this weekend?"

"No." Nick looked as if the doom had come. "I guess she still has the key."

CHAPTER ELEVEN

Detachment

I rushed Nick out the door for his hockey game the following evening. The Book Club was due in half an hour, and I still had to set up the screen porch and put out the food. I arranged a big bouquet of peonies in a flower seller's bucket. I put guest towels in the powder room and ice in the wine cooler. Abby and Macduff followed me into the living room and curled up together on the loveseat. I opened the French doors onto the porch and turned on the lights. I cleaned off the table and put out the salads and canapés. I heard Jane's voice in the back hall. Mac jumped down to greet her. Abby yawned and stretched out to full length.

"How are you doing?" Jane asked. "It's ridiculous that we live so close and we only see each other infrequently."

"The usual nonsense with one of Nick's kids, but otherwise, everything's status quo."

"Which one was it this time?"

"The First Daughter. She took a group of school cronies up to the lake without asking permission. Even Nick was upset this time. He doesn't like strangers using his stuff. That's why we've never put the house into the rental program."

"Did Nick say anything to Deborah?"

"I have no idea. He tends to speak with her from the office— probably to avoid my eye rolling, so they might be babbling at each other every day, for all I know."

"Well, at least he can't blame this episode on you. She was definitely the problem."

"I was just thinking that myself. You have a lot more experience with offspring than I do. What's going on here?"

"I'd say offhand that Deborah is continually reminding you of her precedence with her father and your homes. The 'I was here first' argument. It's a battle that she can never win, though. Pity that she feels compelled to waste her time in this manner."

"What about her inheritance? Is that an issue?"

"Definitely. Not so much with her brother, apparently."

"No. Douglas is genuine. Annoying, childish, and self-centered, certainly, but nevertheless genuine."

"Emma! We're *starving!*"

Dottie and Denise came onto the porch together. "Eliot is still maneuvering her car into position out there." Dottie laughed. "This could be a while."

"How the hell did we pick the one mystery story on the planet with no body?" Eliot exclaimed. She flounced through the door wearing a baby pink suit with a very short skirt. "Oh, goody. Chardonnay."

We all gorged on girl food. "Great appetizers, Em," Dottie announced, her mouth full.

"Let's begin, then," Jane said, picking up her copy of *Gaudy Night*. "Brief plot synopsis?"

"Harriet Vane returns to her Oxford alma mater for a reunion, or gaudy. She is worried about her reception at this gathering, given her rather infamous history since graduating and her narrow escape from hanging for a murder that she didn't commit," Denise volunteered. "However, the professors, or dons, have problems of their own and enlist her aid in solving the mystery of the poison pen slash poltergeist, who is terrorizing the college."

"Well done. Now, mystery aside—the solution to which I felt was rather obvious from the start—what are some of the other issues that Harriet is confronting as the story progresses?"

"There is a lot of discussion about doing one's appointed job, whatever *that* means, regardless of the personal costs," Dottie said.

"Yes, there are several examples of that theme. Harriet, who has been plagued by anonymous letters for years because of her trial, is now being asked to investigate the same sort of distasteful behavior for Shrewsbury College. She is, however, determined to do her job. Lord Peter, who has been proposing marriage to Harriet for five years, agrees to help her stop a criminal who is clearly suffering from what he calls 'devoted love.' He fulfills his promise." Jane paused. "The most obvious example is Miss de Vine's story, which is actually the crux of the entire mystery. She did her job, as well."

"But how was that personal to her?" Eliot demanded. "What risk did she take by discovering the truth about that man Robinson? He wasn't a friend of hers, after all."

"Good question," I said. "Not quite the same thing, is it? In that case, perhaps the risk was the conflict of humanity versus professionalism."

"I think it has to do with the concept of 'womanliness.' Remember that this story takes place a few years before the beginning of World War Two," Jane replied. "Women were in a very different place in society then. A woman's job was to take care of her husband and children. There is discussion among the characters about the 'question' of women's education, for example, and whether one was to be considered a 'womanly woman,' or a 'manly man.' Harriet is in her early thirties, unmarried, and not interested in having children. She graduated with First Class honors in English from Oxford, lived with her lover, was tried for his murder and acquitted, and supports herself by writing mystery stories."

"Hardly a womanly woman by 1935 standards," Denise agreed.

"She makes money from fictional crime, when she was almost executed for a real one," Eliot said.

"Harriet is also grappling with the knowledge that she could be a much better writer than she is, but to expand her literary horizons she must dip into her emotional arsenal. It would take courage," Jane said.

"It's pretty clear by the end of the book that she is prepared to be courageous," Dottie remarked.

"With her personal life, as well as her professional one," I added.

"Jealousy," Eliot said.

"Yes?" Jane prompted.

"Over two hundred women crowded together in a few buildings. There's got to be jealousy."

"The little green monster," Dottie added.

"That is as cruel as the grave," replied Jane.

"Look at Miss Hillyard, the history professor," Eliot continued. "She gets the hots for Lord Peter and then goes after Harriet."

"The dons are described as elderly virgins. Even Harriet suspects that the Poltergeist must be one of them, because she assumes that 'X' is envious of women with sexual experience."

"Lord Peter chides her for that conclusion, remember?" Denise said. "Because she's allowing her personal feelings to cloud her judgment about doing her job."

"Doesn't it bother you that, with all the highly educated women in that college, they still had to call in a man to discover the truth about what was going on?" Eliot demanded.

"That's Annie's point. She tells the dons that they were all jealous of her because she had a husband that she loved. That's why he died."

"What utter nonsense," Eliot scoffed. "Her husband died because he was an unethical academic who got caught cheating on his thesis and lost his job. So, he became a drunk and shot himself. Probably *she* was the one who was jealous of *them*."

I opened my copy of *Gaudy Night*. "In my opinion, the most important passage is Miss de Vine's speech to Harriet at the beginning of the story regarding Detachment. She calls it an unlovable, although rare virtue. Further down, she congratulates Harriet on her ability to discredit those people who are disconcerted by Harriet's unconventional feelings. Tremendous wisdom in those words."

"Certainly," Jane said. "They are words that undoubtedly described Sayers herself. An intellectual, though truly odd woman."

As this was to be our last meeting until September, discussion ranged over various light topics from that point. I went into the kitchen to make coffee and get dessert ready. Jane followed me.

"I am always amazed at the occasional spark of brilliance that can emanate from our Eliot," she commented. "I know she's a lawyer, so I expect her to be more intellectual than she actually is."

"She does mostly criminal litigation, lots of DUI hearings, and motions to suppress. She's quite good."

"I was thinking about our discussion earlier. Is it possible that Deborah is simply jealous of you?"

"Of me? Why should she be? I'm twice her age."

"But you've got the package that most women wish for."

"What do you mean?"

"Brains, looks, talent …."

"Oh, come on, Jane!"

"I'm serious, Emma. You've always been terrible about taking compliments. As I was saying, brains, looks and talent, but mostly because of what we talked about tonight."

"Detachment."

"Precisely. The ability to tune out the world and all its noise. Honesty is part of it, but the real gift is the capacity to know how you feel and what you want, all of the time. Do you realize how unusual that is?"

"I haven't thought about it. It's always been so easy for me."

"For you, it *is*. Do you remember what Miss de Vine says to Harriet about never persuading oneself into appropriate feelings?"

"Yes."

"You never have, have you? You've probably never been jealous a day in your life."

"I think jealousy is the world's biggest waste of emotion."

"You're probably right. But you are one of a very small group of people who actually feels that way. Now, do you see why Deborah might be jealous, not to mention intimidated by such a formidable stepmother?"

"Maybe," I said slowly. "But that doesn't make me like her better."

"Well, it wouldn't, would it?" Jane laughed.

That night, I sat at the desk in my study balancing my checkbook and paying bills. Nick had gone out after the game with his hockey buddies. Mac and Abby, well-behaved for a change, were quietly sharing space on my chaise. I leaned back in my chair and closed my eyes.

I feel as though my entire life is one long episode of Charmed. *By day, I do the usual mundane, ridiculous things. But every morning is a challenge as I frantically try to recall the stream of images from the night before. The colors are becoming more intense, as well. I feel like I'm desperate to cry, but something won't let me. Really cry, as in tor-*

rents that I can't control and can't see through. And sometimes I can't breathe at all, or it comes in short gasps, as if I've been running.

But I think I finally understand what this huge release is supposed to be. We had a tough childhood. Dad was an abusive drunk. He made inappropriate comments about my body, and treated me like a second wife in the house. He was physically abusive as well. This created terrible feelings of conflict for me, and alienated me from my mother, who was clearly jealous, and never protected me from him. Kate, on the other hand, was treated like a normal kid, which explains the tension in our relationship, to this day.

Audrey is still self absorbed and cruel. My first husband cheated on me and left me stranded. I represent women in worse situations every day. How soon before I can move on and rejoin the normal world? I can't be alone in this. These sleep time movies must be very commonplace. But no one wants to be considered barking mad.

The other night, I dreamed that I was back in that squalid apartment in Bridgeport that I had shared with Shawn. He was already gone; I couldn't pay the rent, and I didn't have any heat because I didn't have the money for an oil delivery.

I will never again live in fear like that.

All the dream books tell us to pay careful attention to the symbols and the colors; that if we commit to analyzing the messages, we will grow and evolve as human beings. I hope so. I feel like I have just skipped three grades and have no idea where I am or what I'm doing; that someone else has my schedule, but won't tell me what it is.

Annie buzzed. "Ghost client, John Ambrose, line two."

"Emma? Just wanted you to know that we're all set for next Wednesday evening at seven."

"I've spoken to Patty's lawyer. He said that he hired the medium."

"Ethel Holt. She's a Brit. Very well respected in the field. The state police use her."

"Good. Well, I'll be there." I almost added "with bells on," but restrained myself. "Is Patty allowing the children to be present?"

"They're staying at Patty's with a babysitter. Patty feels that it will be too terrifying for them."

"Hmm. Perhaps she's right this time. I'll see you next week, then."

Annie brought in my mail. "Your mom's on hold."

"Emma, dear?"

"Yes, Mother."

"I was wondering, dear, are you free on Saturday?"

"Free for what, specifically, Mother?"

"Well, dear, I have decided that I desperately need a new light fixture in the kitchen. Would you be willing to drive me to that place in Danbury in the morning?"

"We have a lot on our plates right now, Mother."

"I thought it might be nice to go back to that bistro afterward, for lunch."

"I'm changing barns on Saturday, and it's going to be pretty hectic."

"You could swing up here very easily, couldn't you, dear?"

It was not Audrey's day. "In other words, Mother, I could spend twenty-five minutes in the car to pick you up, then another hour for the round trip to Danbury, then wait the inevitable additional hour it will take you to pick out one ceiling lamp, then lunch, which I'm sure I'll be paying for, and then my return trip to Warwick. Is that what you would characterize as 'swinging by,' Mother?"

Audrey altered her tone. "Well, *really*, dear. What else could you *possibly* have to do all day? It's not as though you have a child to raise, as your sister does."

CHAPTER TWELVE

Séance

I took my first lesson on Joy with Olivia at Lisa and Jack's new barn. I arrived at Lisa's at seven-thirty to get Joy ready. Lisa met me with a muck rake in one hand. "Joy had a good time rolling in her paddock after breakfast, Em," Lisa said, laughing. "She's pretty funny about it. Really grinds both sides of herself thoroughly."

"Looks like she brought a big chunk of the field back with her!" There were even grass clods in her tail. "Do you mind if I use your vacuum?"

"Help yourself. I'm almost done with the stalls. Then, I think I'll take a shower. Just so you know, the framers should be here at about eight to work on the new barn."

"Thanks." I got out my grooming bag and plugged in the horse vacuum. Joy stood patiently while I ran the hose over both sides of her. I began to pick shavings and grass out of her tail with my fingers. Joy had an amazing tail—thick, black hair, and so long it had to be trimmed regularly to keep her from tripping on it. I had just buckled the throat strap on her bridle when Olivia's diesel truck came up the hill and parked next to my car.

"I've already built a little course in the ring," she announced as we walked back down the driveway. I noted the traditional line, diagonal/line, diagonal hunter set up. "We'll do a flat warm-up first and a couple of single cross rails. Then, I want you to do the green line by itself. Trot in, pull her back to the trot after the first X, and trot over the vertical. She needs to learn not to rush down these jump lines."

I concentrated on using my body position, rather than the bit, to get Joy to make the transition to trot after the first cross rail. It required a couple of canter strides, but she did it for me. We trotted over the green vertical at a leisurely pace.

"Loosen up your elbows; your hands are bouncing a little. Otherwise, good. Now, trot in and canter out. Just that line. It should be a nice, quiet six strides."

I relaxed my shoulders, shook out my arms, and trotted back around to the beginning. Joy was perfect. I kept my hands low and even, my back straight, and my eyes up. She popped over the X, cantered her six gentle strides, and calmly jumped the vertical at the other end.

"Excellent!" Olivia exclaimed. "Your right heel came up over the second fence, and I don't want you to release over these little jumps. But great. She's a fast learner, huh? All right, let's try the course. For now, I want you to bring her back to a trot before each line."

Lisa came out of the house, and Mimi, the kitten, followed her down to the ring to watch. Joy and I had a terrific time. I had never done a whole course with her before, and I think she was just as excited as I was. We completed the course three times and then cantered a courtesy circle. "Very impressive, Emma!" Lisa said. "She looked like a hunter."

Olivia laughed. "She takes very good care of her mom; that's for certain."

"She's happy here; that makes all the difference. Thanks, Olivia."

"My pleasure. You've said that this week is bad for you, so I'll school her the next few days. We'll lesson again next week, when you can come again."

Annie buzzed me at four-thirty on Wednesday afternoon. "Judge Schaeffer's clerk is holding for you."

"Ms. Carbury? The judge asked me to inform all counsel in the *Ambrose* matter that he will be attending the, ahem, gathering tonight. As you know, the judge has ordered that the medium is not to receive advance information regarding this file. I have just now emailed to her the address of Mr. Ambrose's house."

Annie followed me to Darien in her car. We arrived at John Ambrose's home at six-fifteen. He was waiting for us at the door. "Mrs. Holt, the medium, isn't due to arrive until the dot of seven," he explained. "That way, no one can claim that the well has been poisoned, so to speak. Let me show you around."

The building was an old farmhouse, situated near the road, with a detached garage at the end of the driveway. The property was several blocks from the Sound, about half an acre of land, and possessed of quite a few large, old trees. "Not too spooky," Annie observed to me, quietly. There was a wide front porch. The big, paneled door opened into a center hall, with two, almost empty rooms on either side. The wallpaper was in poor shape and dated. "We always meant to tear it down and repaint, but it just wasn't a priority," John explained. "Patty took most of the furniture. I haven't gotten around to shopping for new pieces yet." We moved into the kitchen, which was attached to an old fashioned keeping room, and opened out to another porch to the rear of the house. This room was clearly the living space for the children, when they were in residence. There were large baskets filled with toys and books, and a child-sized table and chairs.

The knocker on the front door banged. John excused himself and went out.

"Do you sense anything?" Annie inquired.

"Just your nails digging into my arm."

"Oh, sorry."

Jonelle Bigelow, the Attorney for the Minor Children came in, followed by Judge Schaeffer. "What happens now?" Jonelle asked.

"When everyone's here, we can get going," John explained.

"Do we sit at the dining room table and hold hands?" Annie asked.

"No," replied John with some irritation. "That's completely passé."

Patty Ambrose, and her attorney Philip Bahn, came through. Patty was the Queen Bee type of female that I invariably disliked upon contact. Her lawyer was the male equivalent.

"Mrs. Holt is pulling up now," Bahn announced, looking out the window. It was seven o'clock exactly. "She's just standing there, staring at the house. Good evening, your honor."

"We won't disturb her, then," the judge said.

"Well, I hope you're satisfied, John. You've dragged us all here on your wild ghost chase," Patty snarled, her expensively veneered fangs showing. John wisely kept silent.

"Just how many times have you seen this ghost, Mr. Ambrose?" Phillip Bahn inquired.

I was not going to allow Bahn to corner my client in front of the judge. "We don't know that she's a ghost, actually, do we, John? She might be a spirit."

"What the hell's the difference?" Patty demanded.

"Ghosts are stuck here on this plane. They're very confused about what's going on. They tend to relive their final moments as mortals over and over, and are trapped here until someone like

Ethel sends them on their way," John said. "Spirits have passed to the Other Side. They are, well, free to come and go as they please. They think and act as we do, just on another plane."

We all digested this information. Annie frowned. "So, if she's just a ghost, she wouldn't be such a great babysitter, huh? I mean, she couldn't dial 911 in an emergency."

Ethel Holt came in about three minutes later. I had been expecting a flamboyant character figure in the Hollywood tradition, but she was a petite woman, neatly dressed in a navy pantsuit, with a lavender silk scarf around her neck. She immediately began climbing the front staircase.

"Where the hell is she going?" Patty's shrill voice broke the silence.

"Let's see," the judge replied, and the rest of us followed him to the second floor. Ethel was standing in a small back bedroom. She spoke directly to John. "This house is old. Late eighteen-hundreds."

"Yes," he said. Even if Ethel had been able to peruse the land records, there was no way she could have known which of the men was the owner.

"Your great grandfather built this house, and your family has been here ever since."

"Correct."

"I'm getting something about the sea. Fishing."

John looked at me. I nodded back. I had instructed him not to reveal any unnecessary information to the medium.

"My grandfather was a commercial fisherman."

Ethel walked out into the hall and into a larger room. This one was obviously used by the little boy, Tucker. The wallpaper was new here; jungle animals and palm trees. A mobile of various dinosaurs in primary colors hung over the bookcase. The bed was the shape of a small dinghy. It even had rubber oarlocks.

Ethel sat down. She said the name "LIBBY" quite clearly, and immediately went into a trance.

"Is she going to be sick?" Annie cried.

"Shhh!" Judge Schaeffer replied.

Ethel began to speak, her British accent gone.

"Get her OUT of this house!"

"What does she mean?" Jonelle asked John. John looked grim, but didn't answer.

"Get her OUT! THE CRIB!"

Judge Schaeffer took charge. Except for John, the rest of us stood petrified. "What about the crib?"

Ethel Holt stared straight ahead. Then, abruptly, she raised her hand and pointed it straight at Patty Ambrose. Patty shrieked in fear.

"WHAT does this mean, Mrs. Ambrose?" the judge demanded.

"I DON'T KNOW!" Patty shouted.

"THE SCAR! THE BOY'S SCAR!"

"I've seen the scar!" Jonelle piped up. "On Tucker's forehead. I was told that he fell out of his crib and banged his head, as a baby."

"WHO told you that?" the judge bellowed at her.

"His mother."

"Oh, God, LOOK!" Annie exclaimed, staring at the corner by the dinosaur mobile. A gleam of light appeared and began to grow. The orb swirled, and, as it did, the mobile swayed and began to pick up momentum. Within seconds, the tiny dinosaurs were a blur of color.

The window shade, covered with characters from Winnie the Pooh, was pulled down taut by an invisible hand and then let go. It flew up and whirled around with a snap. Patty Ambrose shrieked again.

"WHAT HAPPENED TO THE CHILD, MRS. AMBROSE?" Judge Schaeffer roared. Tremendous focus. I was ready to run for the nearest mental facility.

Patty dropped to the floor. "His crying! His goddam crying! I couldn't take it anymore! I just couldn't."

The orb swelled. It was now about half the size of a human being. Annie did little more than gulp. My throat was paralyzed. Disconcerting experience for a lawyer.

John remained calm. "So what did you do, Patty?"

"I picked him up. ALL RIGHT! I picked him up, and SMASHED HIM AGAINST THE HEADBOARD!"

The orb hovered quietly for an instant and then disappeared. Ethel Holt stood up and looked around. "Did you get what you needed?" she asked.

"I want to see counsel in my chambers tomorrow morning at nine-thirty, sharp." The judge glared at each one of us and stormed out of the room. Jonelle followed suit.

"No wonder she didn't want the kids here for this," Annie said. "I need a drink."

"Right behind you," I responded. Philip Bahn was supporting his client through the doorway. I looked at John. "You knew, didn't you? You knew all along."

"Of course I knew. I just couldn't prove it."

"Who's Libby?" Annie asked.

"Elizabeth Mary Conway Ambrose. My grandmother," John replied.

"I was wrong," Annie said, her teeth still chattering. "She's the world's best babysitter."

The next evening, I attempted a half hour with my new yoga DVD. I unrolled my green mat on the family room rug and performed a series of stretches, which included cat and cow, modified plank, cobra, crocodile, and downward facing dog. Macduff, feeling left out of the process, edged up alongside and started sniffing my armpit just as I was attempting a dignified version of downward facing dog. I fell over and started laughing. Mac grinned at me and wagged his tail with appreciation. I lay on my back and started to do some abdominal work. Mac hurried over and licked my face. I gave up and decided to clean out the closet in my study.

Although outwardly a tidy person, I had many cluttered drawers, and closets teeming with memorabilia. I pulled out stacks of old magazines, photo albums, ancient backpacks stuffed with school papers, and rubber tubs full of yearbooks and journals from high school and grade school. My sorority album was bulging with pressed corsages and group photos. I was amazed by my beaming face and size-eight figure. I flipped to my senior profile from Ridgefield High: "To make it to law school." No one had ever bothered to tell us how our lives would change once we passed the bar exam. One of my closest friends, Nell Packer, was captain of the girls' cross country team. Angela Hamilton and Stephanie Cramer had both ended up at Ivy League schools.

A pile of grade school notebooks and photos were lining the bottom of one tub. I smiled at a geometry test—the only math I had ever enjoyed, probably because we got to draw with compasses and protractors. I picked up my first real diary. A gift from my grandmother, it was pink, with flowers decorating one side and a locked loop that had long ago disintegrated. I opened it to entries made when I was twelve years old. My parents had rented a cottage in Harwich Port, on Cape Cod.

> Thursday, July 22
> Mom took us to see a play called "The Secret Garden." I loved it! The set was so pretty, and all the actors had English accents. It's by the same lady who wrote "A Little Princess," which is my favorite book. Afterwards, we went for ice cream

and sat outside. Mom says we have to go watch them play tennis tomorrow. I'd rather go to the beach. We had clam chowder for dinner. Kate gets the bed by the window this year. I went to the bathroom, and Dad yelled at me for peeing too loud. I don't think I'm any louder than Kate, but he didn't say anything to her.

Friday, July 23
Tennis was very hot and boring. Mom can never send the ball back to Dad, which makes him yell. We got back home and Kate and I made tuna sandwiches to take to the beach. Dad made a bucket of orange juice and rum. He came in while Kate and I were changing. He said we should make sure to shave in the right places. Kate and I floated on our rafts and went snorkeling, while Mom read her mags and Dad drank and slept. Kate and I were having fun finding shells with two other kids, when Dad came up and told me I was too loud and I couldn't play anymore. So I took my raft back out. Dad yelled that I was too near the rocks.

Saturday, July 24
Kate and I walked up to the market to get some stuff for Mom. Mom said that she's on vacation, and we're big girls now. On the way there we stopped at the library. I got out a book on horses and another book about whales. Kate got three Nancy Drews. I'm reading all about how to curry

a horse. Dad wouldn't let me go down to the beach with my book in my bathing suit alone. He said that boys wouldn't understand how young I am. He made me put on jeans.

Sunday, July 25
It was raining, so Mom took us to the movies yesterday after lunch. Dad was supposed to go, but he got drunk instead. We saw "The Sound of Music." I liked the singing, especially the goat puppets. We stopped in the penny candy store on the way back. Mom bought some salt water taffy. Kate didn't have any money, so I bought some peanut butter fudge for all of us. But when we got back, Dad took it away from me. He said I was very selfish, that I couldn't have any fudge. I had to go to my room, and I couldn't have any dinner. He wouldn't listen to me. He just kept yelling.

I dropped the diary and began to sob. I curled up on the floor by my chaise and cried and cried. My contacts fogged and my nose was completely blocked. Abby came in and sat quietly up against me until I finally stopped.

CHAPTER THIRTEEN

Jealousy

Lisa had a surprise waiting when I drove up to the barn on Friday morning.

"Henry!" Our favorite groom from the old farm.

"Good morning, Mrs. Emma!"

"Jack and I had just talked ourselves into the rationalization that we need help with the horses, when Henry showed up yesterday afternoon and asked for a job," Lisa explained. "He'll be here Monday through Friday all day, and a half day on Saturday."

"Are you still available for body clipping, Henry?"

"Oh, yes."

"Great. I just bought an Oster Clipmaster, and I haven't got a clue about how to use it."

"I will clip Joy today after work."

The perfect barn, *and* the perfect groom. Paradise.

Sally pulled up. We had arranged that the three of us would hack together in the field. I made several trips into the tack room to bring out my gear. The day was already warm, so I zipped on my half chaps over my breeches and grabbed my string-back gloves.

Sally led Alfie from his stall and snapped the cross ties onto his halter.

Mimi, the tiger kitten, strode in, meowed hello, and headed straight for the feed room and her breakfast.

The field was dry and, thankfully, free from rocks and holes. "Ladies, please remember that our neighbors on this side have chickens and that the roosters can be noisy." We walked the horses in both directions for about ten minutes and then picked up a posting trot. I wanted to work on circles, serpentines, and fig-ure eights; Joy and I were both less balanced when tracking left. An eighteen wheel truck lumbered up the long driveway, hauling building materials for the new barn. Joy looked over at it, but stuck to business. "Anyone mind if I start to canter?" Sally said. Lisa and I waited for a few minutes and then asked our girls for the left lead. "This is why I got a horse in the first place," I called to Lisa. She smiled and nodded. Zara and Joy nickered to each other, but kept to reasonable speeds. We did a flying change to the right lead and circled at the other end of the pasture. The feeling of freedom was marvelous, especially after so many months indoors this win-ter. I wrapped my legs around Joy and made sure that my elbows were flexible and moving with the motion of her head. "She looks relaxed, Emma," Lisa remarked as she passed us going in the other direction, "and so do you." I felt relaxed, possibly for the first time in months.

We dismounted in front of the barn. "Mimi's making a nest out of your jacket," Sally yelled back to me as she walked Alfie down to the wash stall. Joy and I looked at Mimi curled up on the bench on top of my green wind-breaker. Suddenly, Joy froze and started snorting. Then I saw it. Mimi wasn't alone. She had brought a companion in from the garden—a garter snake, which was almost exactly the color of my jacket and about a foot long.

I reacted as any other red-blooded American girl would have

under the circumstances. "HENRY!" I shrieked. I bent poor Joy around like a pretzel and ran out the barn door, dragging her by the reins. Henry appeared with a weed whacker in one hand, just as Lisa rode up on Zara. I explained the nature of the calamity. Henry disappeared into the barn and emerged a minute later, the offensive creature dangling from the end of a muck rake. Mimi followed closely behind, clearly indignant.

"Good thing that jacket is machine washable," I said.

"Was it dead?" Lisa asked, a tad green herself.

"I'm not sure. I didn't really give it close scrutiny. Good first day, huh, Henry?" I asked when he had returned from the dumpster.

"Oh, yes!" Henry grinned. "I am very happy to be here!"

According to my reference books, snakes were symbolic of wisdom, grounding, and healing, and because they shed their skin, of transformation and renewal. Cats were representative of feminine energy. I couldn't find a meaning for jacket, but green was the color of healing.

I invited Kate for a picnic on the beach. We found a spot near the edge of a low dune and spread out our big towel. I handed her a turkey and avocado wrap, and she poured the ice tea.

"Reminds me of all those summers on Cape Cod," she said, looking around. "This really is a nice stretch of sand for a state park."

I decided to bite the bullet. If my sister thought I was crazy, I could always blame Audrey.

"I came across my old pink diary a few nights ago."

"Audrey always wanted to know where you kept the key."

"Do you remember that last vacation in Harwich Port?"

"That was the year we had the hurricanes, wasn't it? I remember being stuck in the cottage for days, doing puzzles because the old TV never worked. You'd be reading; Audrey would be complaining."

"And Dad would be drinking."

"Do you know, I don't recall ever seeing the man eat," Kate replied. "I can visualize him now, elbows on the table, that sagging jaw, blathering on about nothing while the rest of us had dinner. And then Audrey, who never had the sense to shut up, would bait him about something, and he would attack."

"Yes. And I usually got the first strike."

"I know. I never understood why you loved him so much. He was so tough on you."

I felt my stomach drop. "You were always his favorite."

Kate sighed. "And I loved it, I have to confess. You were the A student, the star athlete, the artist, the tower of strength. You had a take charge personality. I got off on being Daddy's little girl."

"Do you remember the time you locked yourself in the bathroom in the Brooklyn apartment, and Dad just assumed that I had done it? He threw me out onto the landing, slammed the door, and I had nowhere to go but up on the roof. Can you imagine what the Connecticut Department of Children and Families would say about that now? I was what? Eight? And once you got out of the bathroom, and came to get me, he didn't even apologize. There were so many instances like that. He'd get drunk, and then try to kick my bedroom door in. Or he'd ram me up against a wall and punch the air over my head, hollering 'You're through!' I always did wonder what the hell he meant."

"Audrey told me that she was afraid he'd drive you crazy."

I stared at her. "When did she tell you that?"

"Around the time that Shawn left you. She thought that was why you'd made such a dysfunctional marriage, because of the way Dad treated you."

"But she never tried to stop him. She'd just retreat to her room and read magazines."

"I know."

"I've been doing research on child abuse and incest. The experts all say that abused children tend to blame the silent parent, who didn't intervene, rather than the abusing parent, who at least paid attention to the child, however negative the contact might have been. I'm only realizing now that the source of my bitterness isn't aimed at Dad, because I always knew he was sick, but at Audrey, who did nothing to stop him when he hurt me."

"I think it was more than that, Em," Kate said, sadly. "I think Audrey was jealous of you."

"Why?" I asked, surprised.

"Because Dad always went to you if there was a problem, even when we were little. You were more like a short adult than a kid. Then you two would laugh at Audrey, as though you both had your own private club, and we weren't included. It bugged her. It bugged me." Kate admitted.

"And yet he never cut me any slack."

"Like I said, I was his little girl. You were more like a spouse in the middle, or the other woman, or something. As a mother, I can see now how damaging that must have been to you."

"The comments about my body were the worst. My upper arms were too heavy, or I wasn't allowed to wear that jumpsuit, remember?"

"The one that was so hour-glassy. But you wore it anyway," Kate grinned.

"Then he'd tell me how tough Audrey was to be married to, and wouldn't I advise her about her makeup, and her choice of colors for her clothes. You're right, I was the little woman to him."

"I'm sorry, Em."

"Kate, I've been having dreams."

"What about?"

"Our childhood. My marriage to Shawn. I notice that whenever I feel shaky or worried, which is most of the time lately, I'm either back in the Brooklyn apartment, or later in Audrey's house in Ridgefield. Sometimes I've returned to the Bridgeport apartment with Shawn. He's just run out on me, and I can't pay the rent, so once again I'm putting all my belongings in storage, and living in boarding situations with strangers, for three years, while working two jobs. Other times it's just symbols. This has been going on for months. I've been using books and the internet to figure out what they mean. Buildings, cars, colors, animals, airports—even a mummy. A few dreams actually came true."

"Wow. Is this since you saw the psychic?"

"It started before that, but after my reading, they really began to escalate."

"What do you think is going on?"

"Honestly? I feel like I'm in some kind of emotional crisis. But not like the kind you see in movies. I'm totally functional in the normal world. I can still practice law and do the laundry. But everything seems a little out of focus. It's as if the rest of the world is watching sports and shopping, and I'm floating around in a daze."

"I won't suggest that you get some help. I know what you think about therapists."

"Right." I rolled my eyes. "The first thing they do is refer you to a shrink who puts you on a pill. Then, of course, you need more visits and more pills so they can collect your insurance and make their malpractice payments. But no one actually ever gets any better. Why? The patients are so semi-embalmed that they don't know the bloody difference. No thanks. I'll figure this out for myself. By doing dream research and yoga. Talking about it helps a lot."

"But you think that this is happening now for a reason?"

"I think that I'm being prepared for something, and, in order to deal with it, I have to clear out my past, so I can change how I react to personal attacks."

Kate grinned. "You always were a she-bear when someone got in your way. Really volatile."

"Now I understand why. Years of abuse. Was it so enjoyable for him as a kid that he felt the need to share the fun? That's just sick."

"Exactly. And don't forget Audrey's contribution. I may not have gotten slammed by Dad, but I've had my share of Audrey's mouth. She just loves to bait people, and then sit back and watch them react." She grinned. "But you're going to work it through and put it behind you. The pattern ends here."

"At least now I know why I never had children. I was always afraid that I'd pass on the family legacy."

That night I dreamed that I'm back in my parents' house in Ridgefield. Audrey is trying to poison me, but I grab the huge syringe from her just in time. I kiss Dad on the forehead, hurl a stinging rebuke to my dear mother, get into my packed Audi, and make my escape.

Then, Abby is in a standoff with a large red fox. They are both snarling and dripping saliva. I pick up my terrier and the fox backs off.

Finally, I'm on a plane that is landing in a field. We taxi over a narrow bridge to another field. As we disembark, the flight attendant tells me that I'll need a passport to be permitted on the next leg of the journey, which is overseas. I worry that I've left my purse on the plane, but the flight attendant brings it out to me.

Kisses were an acknowledgement. Foxes were symbolic of someone who was sly or clever and were usually indicative of a person who was adept at self protection and playing head games. A bridge, like a crossroad, represented an important life transformation that may involve choices and decisions. Fields were open, fertile places and had to do with personal growth and the freedom to express one's own nature. The passport probably meant permission to change direction and explore a new life. The purse could be either femininity or identity. Travel by air was usually about spirituality and evolving consciousness.

There was a manila envelope from Laura waiting for me on my desk the next morning. Inside was a brochure that was entitled *Reiki, Aromatherapy, and Creative Visualization for Balance and Health*, Marilyn Peterson, RN. There was a short note from Laura: Hi Em. I met this woman at the barn yesterday. She's a Reiki Master and a Clinical Aromatherapist. She works with horses and dogs, as well as humans. I thought this might be a good alternative for you. No drugs! Love Laura.

I started reading. Reiki is a Japanese word, meaning Universal Life Force Energy. It is a hands-on healing method that works to create balance in the physical, emotional, and spiritual levels of healing. Aromatherapy is the use of essential oils through inhalation, bathing, or direct application to the skin. When blended together, the therapeutic effects of these oils work to restore balance in the mind and spirit, and stimulate the body's natural ability to heal itself. Used in conjunction with creative visualization, the recipient will experience powerful, positive life changes.

I picked up the phone and made an appointment for the following week.

"You all are aware of the fact that I went to prep school with Senator Armstrong," Basil remarked at the next partner's meeting. "His wife was a passenger in a rather serious accident a few years ago, and William Armstrong has asked this firm to take over the file."

"Where did the accident occur?" Ed asked.

"On Interstate 91, just outside of Cromwell."

"Is there a trial date?"

Basil referred to his legal pad. "Not yet. We're on stand-by, which means that jury selection may begin soon. The defendant is represented by Posner and Underwood, in New Haven."

"I'm sure I'll be able to move some things around, so I'm available," David announced, a smug look on his face.

"No need, David. Emma and I will be trying this case." Basil turned to me. "You and I will be meeting on this as soon as possible."

"Was there something you'd like to say, David?" Mr. McCook asked.

"No. I guess not."

"That's all then."

That night I managed to get Nick to agree to have sex with me. "It's been months," I purred. "I really miss you."

We were standing in the master bedroom. I lit a few candles, and a Mozart CD was playing. I was wearing my favorite midnight blue silk negligee. I walked up to Nick with my arms open, and watched in dismay as he deliberately sat down and removed his shoes. He then stood up, took off his clothes and very quickly jumped on the bed, and under the covers. I slowly followed suit. He wasn't watching me. He was looking at the clock on the bedside table.

I tried to kiss him. He pushed me away. "I want your mouth on me," he said. "You're so good at it." I sighed, and moved down to his crotch. Ten minutes later, he got up and went into the bathroom.

That night I dreamed that Nick and I are in bed. There are hundreds of pills and capsules in a variety of colors, spread out all over the duvet. I am stuffing them by the handful into my mouth. In the corner by the window, a swarm of hornets is flying from a hole in a table and forming a black cloud near the ceiling.

CHAPTER FOURTEEN

Kayak For One

I stopped the car by the gate and got out to get the mail. Our snoopy neighbor, Annette, was walking by with her pug. Mac and Abby came to attention in the back seat.

I kept an eye on the pug. He was much too interested in my right leg.

"Seen anything of our celebrity recently?" Annette asked.

"If you mean Clifford Wells, then no, I haven't."

"He's had that skinny blond at his place a lot. Overnights. I wonder if he plans to marry her," she mused.

"I really have no idea."

"I read in the papers that his divorce finally went through."

"Good to know."

"Well, I need to get my darling Pepe his dinner."

Monday morning, I met with Basil Noles in the office library to go over the Armstrong matter. Annie had spent the better part of the week making copies of everything and assembling trial notebooks. She had neatly tabbed all the relevant sections: pleadings, motions, disclosures of experts, interrogatories, depositions, medical reports, and photos.

I flipped to one of the pictures of the car accident victim, Mrs. Armstrong, which was taken right after her arrival at the hospital.

"Oh, my God!"

Basil grinned. "I take it that you've found the snapshots of our client."

"Who took these? They're outrageous!"

"Her loving husband, my classmate."

"Are you planning to show them to the jury?"

"I think so, yes."

"This woman is topless," I said in a flat tone. "And obese. Does the Senator imagine that he's going to get a loss of consortium award from the jury by embarrassing his wife this way?"

"He wanted to get evidence of the bruise left by the seatbelt. To show the force of the impact."

"They couldn't have used drapes? He wasn't in the car, right? So, he gets the call that his wife has been in an accident and is in the emergency room, and his first thought is to grab a camera and whip off her blouse?"

"I agree that there are good reasons not to introduce these photos at the trial."

I scanned the medical records. "It says here that Mrs. Armstrong weighed two hundred and forty pounds at the time she was admitted. Her height is five-foot-four. She is claiming back injuries, two surgeries. Wearing a back brace for six months."

"Wait till you see it. More like a suit of armor in white plastic."

"Another exhibit, no doubt. My concern is that the jury takes one look at this woman and tells her that if she wasn't overweight, she'd be running marathons by now."

"You're not alone."

"Who's the judge?"

"Lombardi."

"Oh, no." A brilliant jurist, but with the social skills of a seventh grader. "I can't wait for this pre-trial."

"It's scheduled for the end of July. I just got the notice."

"How far apart are the numbers?"

"The defense has offered forty thousand. The client wants more than ten times that much."

"Both offers are ridiculous."

"Agreed. We'll arrange to meet with the surgeon before the pre-trial."

July Fourth on Pequot Lake was the busiest holiday of the year. The boat landing was always packed with people unloading canoes, kayaks, sailboats, and even catamarans. I was determined to do some kayaking that weekend.

"Our canoe is perfectly good, Emma. I don't understand this new obsession of yours."

"I'd hardly call it an obsession, Nick. We need two people to haul the canoe down to the water, and it's too cumbersome for one person to paddle alone. I want a little kayak, so I can just throw it in and take off."

"I think they have rentals at the Recreation Office."

I called. "Yes, Mrs. Bennington. The rate is twenty dollars a day, and the boat must be back here by four p.m."

"Can't I just rent one for the whole weekend?"

"No, that's not possible. We only have daily rates."

How ridiculous. "Nick," I hollered through the screen door to the deck, "I'm going into town."

"OK. Why?"

"I'm buying a kayak."

I love outdoor sports stores. There's something marvelously freeing about high tech camping and boating equipment. It must be how Julie Andrews felt, twirling around on the top of that mountain and singing.

The young salesman admitted that he was terrified of swimming.

"But you still kayak? That's pretty brave of you. What if you flip over?"

"I try not to," he replied.

"Well, I'm not looking for anything too fancy. I don't need a sea kayak with a rudder, and I'm certainly not interested in white water. Just something easy so I can paddle around the lake."

"This little boat is perfect for you," he said, directing me to a dark green kayak with yellow deck rigging. "Seven feet long. Weighs thirty-five pounds, so you can lift it yourself. Very stable and maneuvers easily. It's designed for lakes and quiet rivers. You could even take it out on protected ocean bays. There's a storage compartment, and bow and stern deck lines. Go ahead and get in. The seat is comfortable."

"It is! And I've got plenty of leg room in here."

"The best part is, we're having a sale, so I can give you twenty percent off."

"As long as we can get it in the Volvo wagon, you've got a deal."

"What else do you need? Spray skirt? A paddle, a PFD?"

He measured my arm length and found me a beautiful wood paddle. "They have more flexibility than the plastic," he explained. I tried on a red PFD and added that to my pile. "I don't suppose you carry these for dogs? I have two terriers who love to jump out of boats." He showed me their selection of canine preservers. I picked out a small and a medium in yellow. I thought about my painting gear and added a couple of ten-liter watertight bags. Finally, he located a black spray skirt that would fit the cockpit.

Nick helped me unload my new toy. I sent him over to the

Recreation Office to get a boat sticker, while I adjusted the foot braces and attached the kneepads. Feeling a little excited, I strapped on my amphibian sandals.

"OK, Abby, we're in business." Abby looked at the kayak, and then back up at me. "I know that yellow is not your best color, but the only other choice we had was bright orange. Now the trick will be to get you, the paddle, and the boat down to the water in one trip."

"Need a hand?" Nick asked.

"No, thanks. I want to make sure I can do this alone, in case you're not here." I had Abby by her leash in my left hand. I hooked the two pieces of the paddle into their holders on either side of the kayak and then picked the boat up by the cockpit. Down the slope we went to the launch area.

"I'm impressed!" Our neighbor Holly called from her deck.

"Thanks, but the tough part is to come!" I replied. I tucked Abby under my left arm and pulled the kayak into the shallow water. I stepped in and sat down. I released the two pieces of the paddle and connected them. Abby perched comfortably on the seat in front of me and looked straight ahead.

"Isn't that a little dangerous?" Nick asked. "What if you roll?"

"I can lift it to drain easily and then flip it back over. This isn't a big boat. Abby will float."

"Can you move your arms with her in your lap?"

"I don't know. Let's find out. Sure, as long as she stays down."

It was a perfect summer day. There were plenty of people splashing and screaming at the beach. One little girl on the float noticed us and alerted everyone else. "Look, look. Doggie in the kayak!" Motorboats were prohibited near the beach, so I only had to dodge the human propelled obstacles, mostly canoes. I decided to steer around the big island and explore some of the coves on the north end of the lake. Many of them were so shallow that it was difficult to navigate a canoe through, and often, trees had fallen over or vegetation had grown up from the bottom. One dead pine created a tunnel. I had to duck as we passed underneath.

Abby spotted the baby loon before I did. It was alone, sitting in the water in the shadow of a boulder that projected from the eastern shore of the island. Where were its parents?

I had some trouble keeping Abby seated. She had very little play in her leash, but even thirteen pounds leaning to one side can disturb the weight distribution of a kayak. I shifted a little to port to steady us. "Sit down, Abby; you're scaring him!" Of course, she paid no attention. Then, I heard one of the adult loons. It was a distress cry coming from way over on the other side of the big island. The baby loon answered feebly. I started to panic. Raccoons and turtles were everywhere in these islands. The little bird wouldn't have a chance.

If you turned your back on a horse in a paddock and walked away, he almost always followed you to the gate. It was worth a try. I dug the left blade of the paddle into the water and did an about-face. Abby tried to scramble around to keep her eye on the loon, but was frustrated by the movement of the paddle. Would he come after us? I looked toward the stern. Yes! I went along slowly, softly dipping the paddle left, right, left again, without too many awkward movements, all the while scanning for mom and dad. We were definitely getting warm. The cries were louder, and the other parent responded quite close to us. I saw the second baby loon first, swimming further out. Our little guy called out just as one of the adults emerged by a group of dogwoods on the edge of the island. Abby and I slipped quietly away.

Our new neighbors were waiting for us at the launch area. The wife was the skinny, controlling type. She spoke only in a fierce whisper and dumped most of the dirty work on her flabby, thoroughly whipped husband.

"Dogs aren't allowed in the lake," he announced, belly and chins swaying in indignation.

"She's not in the lake, she's in the boat."

"It's unsanitary," spat the wife, arms folded and scowl deep.

"Only if she's actually in the water," I replied, holding Abby under my left arm and picking up the paddle with my other hand.

"If we see this again, we will report you to security," she hissed.

"And if I see *you* again, I'm going to bludgeon you to death with my paddle." I smiled my most charming and proceeded up the path to our deck.

"Not one of our better weekends," Nick commented when I told him the story.

"Have we even formally met these horrors?" I asked.

"I have. They were at the meeting back in May."

"Did they say anything to you?"

"Just a general complaint about dogs to the West Cove committee. A fairly lengthy one, actually."

"Good."

"There weren't any witnesses to this, er, exchange, were there?"

"No. It's their word against mine."

"What a relief. I'll make that argument to the judge at your bail hearing."

It was possible to avoid one's own mother for only so long. Dodging phone calls would provide temporary deliverance, certainly. But Audrey was as inexorable as a runaway train. I was forced to meet her for lunch in Ridgefield on the following Wednesday.

"Lovely to see you, dear. It really has been *such* a long time."

"Yes, Mother."

"Well, everything on the menu looks simply divine. Did you say that lunch was going to be your treat today, dear?"

"I didn't, but of course, have whatever you like."

"Too kind of you, darling. Here comes the girl. That smoked

salmon and caviar appetizer looks absolutely marvelous. I'll start there. And then, I think, the seafood crepe. Will you share a bottle of champagne with me, dear?"

"I'm meeting with a new client this afternoon, Mother. I'll have the vichychoise and the grilled vegetable salad. And another ice tea, please. Kate tells me that you have decided to cut back on buying Hannah's savings bonds this year."

"As I explained to your sister, I intend to pay down my credit cards. I *am* on a fixed income, you know, dear."

"I think she'd be more impressed with your decision if you hadn't just booked a cruise to Alaska with your church cronies."

"I'm entitled to enjoy myself, Emma, dear. You and Nick have certainly done a fair amount of traveling in the last few years."

"We are also somewhat more generous with Hannah than twenty-five dollar savings bonds for her birthday that cost what? Twelve-fifty each?"

"You're being especially rude today, dear. Perhaps we should change the subject."

"What subject would you prefer, Mother?"

"Perhaps you have heard, dear, that my friend Betty Lynn's husband has just died."

"No, I hadn't. I'm very sorry. When is the funeral?"

"Oh, I thought I'd just go to the viewing tomorrow night, dear. These things can be so very distressing, you know."

I maintained a detached demeanor.

"That's usually true, Mother. But wasn't Betty Lynn extremely supportive of you when Dad died?"

"I suppose so, dear."

"Well, don't you think that a little reciprocation is in order here?"

"Hardly, dear. Betty Lynn has been left in a very secure position financially."

"So she needs less friendship than you do?"

"She needs less of everything than I do, dear. Your soup looks heavenly. May I have just a tiny spoonful?"

Kate called me the following evening.

"She talked me into taking her to the viewing."

"How on earth did she do that?"

"She's going to continue Hannah's savings bonds, or so she says."

"Seems like a heavy price to pay for twelve-fifty a year."

"You don't know the half of it."

"Oh, tell, tell."

"I picked Audrey up at the house at five and drove her the whole two miles to Kenwick funeral home."

"Where we had Dad's festivities."

"Right. We walked into the designated parlor. Betty Lynn was greeting people at the door. She seemed more subdued than usual, but perfectly composed and gracious. Audrey suffered herself to be hugged. The usual murmurs of thank you for coming ensued. Audrey then glanced over at the, uh, display area and said to me, quite audibly, 'How long do you think we have to stay, dear?' I was practically frozen with shame."

"Did Betty Lynn hear this?"

"There's just no way that she didn't. We were in that room all of fifteen minutes. I don't think Audrey even signed the guest book. And, Em, she didn't send flowers."

"For one of her oldest friends?" I yipped, horrified.

"I know. Do you think we should send some?"

"Good idea. Sign the card from all of us, and I'll pay half."

That night I dreamed that I am on the deck of a boat, and the boat is slowly sinking. I keep yelling for Abby; it is very important that I find her. No one else is with me. I clutch Abby to me as the boat slips quietly into the water and disappears. Everything around me is very still.

The lawyer from Massachusetts had an engaging demeanor. "Marital Mediation," he began, "uses the mediation process to keep couples together. It provides couples with a place to talk, without the psychotherapy involved in counseling. The focus is on the future, rather than the past. The clients recognize their own issues, and they create their own solutions. The process of Marital Mediation employs mediation techniques to open and improve lines of communication, help couples address areas of friction in their relationship, and develop guidelines that focus on the behavioral changes each will make in order to lessen future conflict. Marital Mediation succeeds if a couple is willing to make a good faith effort to reach an agreement. There is no legal obligation to agree. Any commitment to mediation is voluntary."

A therapist in the front row raised her hand. "If I draft an agreement for my patients, isn't that the illegal practice of law?"

"Big time," Denise whispered to me.

"Probably, but remember that I'm not admitted in Connecticut," replied Attorney Cox.

The therapist bristled. "So basically what you're saying is that lawyers can engage in marriage counseling, but therapists can't draft agreements."

Denise nudged me, and I grinned.

"As I said, marital mediation, like divorce or civil, or even criminal mediation, utilizes the same tools. Define what the parties want, define what the parties are afraid of, reframe the issues, and enter into an agreement. The process has nothing to do with therapy."

"Why would a couple prefer to mediate with a lawyer, rather than a therapist?" One of the lawyers asked.

"First, because many people are shy of committing to counseling. They don't want to dig around in the past, and rehash old behaviors. They want to focus on the future, and new methods of communication." Arthur Cox smiled. "This is especially true of men. Second, because lawyers are trained, and licensed to draft agreements, and third, because if questions arise regarding the law, a lawyer can answer them. Let's move on to the process itself."

"A couple jointly hires a mediator, or neutral facilitator. They sign a Mediation Fee Agreement. During a series of meetings the parties identify their issues, and work out a mutually satisfactory plan to address these issues. They may exchange financial information, and agree to the sharing of responsibilities. Each partner is free to consult with a lawyer, financial planner or therapist at any time. Once a meeting of the minds is reached, depending on the wishes of the couple, the parties may agree on an informal, unwritten understanding. In the alternative, I may draft an Agreement for each party to review with his or her advisor before signing."

"In your seminar packets you'll find some sample issues to address in Marital Mediation. I thought that I would highlight the most common issues for you today, which tend to be finances, housework and raising the children."

"If one of the partners is a full time homemaker, I guarantee you that the conflicts between them are arising from at least two of the three issues that I just mentioned. He or she wants to be assured that his or her contribution to the marriage, although not remunerative, is valued by the other spouse."

"The problem with my marriage in a nutshell," I whispered to Denise. "And I make money."

"This sounds like a post nuptial agreement," remarked another lawyer.

"But much more detailed!" Cox replied. "I've drafted contracts whereby the parties agree to speak respectfully to each other, and to listen to each other, or cash exchanges hands. I've also written contracts that include provisions regarding the in-laws, and how much time will be spent with each set, especially during the holidays." There was laughter. "That issue is surprisingly popular."

"Are you thinking what I'm thinking?" Denise asked, at the break.

"That it would be possible to ditch divorce all together and just do this, and maybe some civil? Definitely!"

Denise looked starry-eyed. "No more court, not even for uncontested divorces. Heaven."

I was weeding my back perennial border when I heard a thud against the screen door of the gazebo. A barn swallow was sitting on the chaise inside; several feathers on his right wing were hanging askew. How did he get in? The vents in the cupola were too small. I decided to take action before the bird made a mess on my upholstery. I propped the heavy door open with a chair, and tried to shoo him out. He skimmed over the top of my head, and perched on the green bistro table. I tried again. This time the poor thing tried to fly through the screened window, and thwarted, he landed on the wrought iron floor lamp, breathing hard. I picked the lamp up near the base, and gently shook it out the open door. This time, the swallow was able to make his escape.

CHAPTER FIFTEEN

Reiki and Aromatherapy

Typically, by the end of July, my yen to garden has diminished almost entirely. All the local nurseries were running huge sales on perennials and bushes, and there was not a potted annual to be had in Fairfield County. It was time to pull the last weeds out of the borders and have a gin and tonic in the shade.

However, I did manage to pick up some great bargains on partial-sun to sun plants on Saturday morning.

The afternoon was dedicated to digging holes for my new additions. I was looking more than a little wilted and dirty when Clifford Wells strolled down our driveway to say hello. Really, men are amazing when it comes to timing. I brushed a fly out of my face and attempted to appear dignified.

"Emma! I'm impressed! It's a bit warm to be doing this kind of work, isn't it?"

"Quite," I replied with a grin.

"I know this is very short notice, but Camille and I were thinking about grilling outside tonight, and we wondered if you and Nick were free to join us."

"We'd love to. Thank you, Cliff. Do I have time to take a shower?"

"Absolutely. Shall we say about six o'clock?"

Two hours later, we were comfortably arranged in steamer chairs on Cliff's veranda, facing the pool. I had determined to make up for my afternoon troll-like appearance and had arrived attired in a new dress—pale green, sleeveless, with sparkly embroidery and side slits. Camille looked ravishing in shell pink, her tiny, size-four feet in delicate bone sandals. She handed me a margarita in a frosted glass.

"Tell us about your visit to Bath," I said, after taking that first refreshing gulp. "Did you see all the sights?"

"Have you been there?" she asked.

"Once," Nick replied. "For two days. But that was at least seven years ago."

"What I remember most is all the honey-colored limestone," I said.

"I took her around to all the usual tourist attractions," Cliff remarked. "Royal Crescent, of course. Pulteney Bridge, Royal Victoria Park."

"The Pump Rooms," Camille added. "I'm a fan of Jane Austen."

"So is Emma," Nick said. "Did you see the Roman Baths?"

"Yes," Camille replied rather abruptly.

"They're a little spooky," I agreed. "Interesting, but I couldn't wait to get out of there. Did you see anything else of the West Country?"

"We spent an afternoon at our family estate in Devon. Didn't happen upon any ghosts, though," Cliff said, grinning. "Just lots of tapestries and antiques."

"That was lovely," Camille brightened again. "The family has some marvelous old silver."

"Right. The grill looks just about ready. I have salmon and tuna steaks. I also have New York strip steaks. Shall I put it all on?"

"Excellent!" Nick said with enthusiasm. I poured myself another margarita.

"Cliff, I have to admit, I am just dying to see the inside of your pool house. Do you mind if I wander over there?"

"I'll take you," Camille said quickly. I waited for her to refill her glass, wondering what she wanted to say to me.

The structure had been built about twenty years ago in the style of the main house, sided in white clapboard, with a front porch supported by columns, and tall windows. The interior was one large room, with a compact kitchen and bar, flanked by two smaller changing rooms, and two full baths. The color scheme was my favorite—soothing blues and greens. Draperies in blue and white stripe brushed the hardwood floor. Camille allowed me time to glance at all the splendors and then made a point of sitting on the overstuffed sofa in the main room. I took the hint and parked on the green toile armchair across from her.

She came right to the point. "I had the opportunity to meet Cliff's ex-wife while we were in London," she began. "She's a beautiful woman. Like you, she's a statuesque brunette, athletic, very direct."

"Was she direct about anything in particular?"

"Yes. Cliff had taken the boys shoe shopping at Church's, and Daphne invited me to tea at Fortnum and Mason. I thought it very civilized of her."

"Very."

"We were served the traditional three-tier array of sandwiches and scones. She poured out. And then she talked. She wanted me to know, in her lovely, cultured, Queen's English, just how much of a shit Clifford truly is."

"Sounds as though you had a delightful time."

"My question to you is this: do you come across this kind of thing regularly in your work? Was Daphne's behavior fairly common?"

"Definitely. Nick's daughter did almost exactly the same thing to me. The day I met her. Nick went out to pick up Chinese. The car door had barely slammed, and her mouth was off and running."

Camille looked more relaxed. "Oh, good. I haven't ever married, you see. No frame of reference."

"Never underestimate the power of jealous bitterness." I paused. "Having said that, I've also found that very often there is no smoke without fire. In my experience, wives tend to be right on point when it comes to their husbands. They've had years to see through the charm, I suppose. Does Cliff know about your tea, by the way?"

"No," she replied, standing up. "Daphne called me at the hotel. I'll take what you've said under advisement. Shall we rejoin the men?"

After dinner, we took a stroll around Cliff's new garden. The landscape architect had staked out the designated area for the proposed fountain, which was situated with a view directly across the street to our front gate.

"We'll get cracking on your application with the town in September, Cliff," Nick said.

"That's good news. I'd really like to have everything done before the ground freezes."

"The garden is just glorious, Cliff." I looked around with appreciation at the hollyhocks and delphinium. The herb garden was attractive, with its various topiary shapes. "Very English."

"Thanks. This bench was shipped over from London last week."

We said our goodbyes at the driveway and walked back home.

"Nick," I said thoughtfully, "you know how you like to call your house 'Terrier Hall'?"

"Yes. Why?"

"Well, what if we officially named it that? Had a little sign made for the gate?"

"Wouldn't that be pretentious?"

"For this neighborhood? Besides, three of the properties on Stone Meadow Road are already named."

"That's true. All right. Do whatever you like about a sign. Will it have a terrier on it?"

"Of course. Mac and Abby will love it."

Kate called after lunch the next day. "I'm curious about these Reiki sessions you're having," she said. "A few of the women in my Pilates class were talking about it last week. Do you feel any different?"

"You wouldn't believe how fast this stuff works! I've had three meetings with Marilyn, and I've cleared out our childhood, and my first marriage."

"Are you using the oils, too? I've seen ads from natural body places that extol the virtues of peppermint and grapefruit and lavender."

"She mixes the oils depending on what I'm working on releasing that session. The oils all have different properties, and apparently my body tells her what I need each time, with something called muscle testing. I don't really understand how she does it, but I've been letting go of a lot of emotional sludge. So far, the oils come in little jars with roller balls. Marilyn gives me detailed drawings and instructions on where and how to apply them. The oils help to support me while I'm doing this energy work, which is really very powerful."

"What's the Reiki like?"

"It's a very strong healing energy that comes through Marilyn's hands. There's actually an odor, like garlic, as she starts to 'cook.'

I'm on a massage table, in my clothes, sometimes under a blanket. She has me do breathing exercises very similar to the ones we practice in yoga, and then we work on creative visualizations while she applies the Reiki, usually through my head, but sometimes she moves around the whole table. The point is to move the bad energy out, and the healing energy in."

"What are you seeing?"

"It's different every time, but she always has me start in a garden that I've created as my safe place. It has an iron scroll gate, and the plants are what you'd see on Nantucket: roses and hydrangeas, lavender and ornamental grasses. It's very serene, with a weathered wood staircase down to the beach. I get acclimated there, and then off I go on that session's adventure."

"And this is how you release the past?"

"Yes! So far, I've had conversations with Dad, Audrey, and Shawn. I say what I need to say to them, the cord between us is dissolved, and I let them go with compassion. In Dad's case, I was able to feel love as he walked away."

"Have you gotten to Nick yet?"

"No, and I'm a little worried about that."

"Why?"

"According to Marilyn, we all tend to follow patterns of behavior, over and over until we honor and release our past pain. I've attended enough family law seminars to know that, statistically, second marriages have an even higher rate of failure than first marriages do."

"The gunk just gets recycled in round two?"

"Exactly. Nick and I have *so* many issues. His self-centeredness, his kids, his control of the finances. My anger, of course," I paused. "The sex, or lack thereof."

"I've never heard you talk about this before, Em! I've always wondered. You and Nick seem friendly to each other, and you have a pleasant lifestyle, but that's it. I'm not surprised to hear that there are problems in the bedroom."

"The irony is that Shawn and I were at it like rabbits all the time. Then he cheated. Did I marry the one man I knew would never have any interest in cheating? I don't know. Stay tuned for further developments."

"This sounds a little scary."

"It feels scary until I walk into Marilyn's room. She exudes peace and balance, and I seem to tune into her frequency right away. The process is actually very soothing, and I always leave amazed at the progress we've made in just an hour or so." I took a deep breath. "And I *had* to do something, Kate. I felt like I was falling apart, and no one else was aware of it."

"Well, I'm proud of you. You have a lot of courage, and if your trip to the psychic started it all, then I'm happy to take part of the credit."

"Marilyn explains life like this: we're all here to play roles and learn from them, which is pretty much what Ingela the psychic told me as well. The problem is, we're actors on a gigantic stage, playing to an even larger audience, but we have no idea what's in the script—which Marilyn says we wrote before we got here. Dreams are clues, I guess. So we flounder around, get shoved into position by invisible directors, get stuff handed to us by invisible prop masters, and the tables are turned by invisible stage hands. There's no way out of it, and there's no way to change it. At the end of show, when we go back Home, as Marilyn calls it, we get our review."

"I think I've had this nightmare. I may have been naked."

"But my question is this—why bother? Why sweat it so much? If our lives are going to happen anyway, and we're meant to just feel whatever it is and move on, why not just do it, and stop whining?"

"Your question is probably the answer. But most people do seem to prefer the drama of living in constant emotional chaos. Look at Audrey."

Annie dropped a copy of a Web page on my desk the next morning.

"The Sign Solution?" I asked. "Are they any good?"

"They did the one that hangs outside this building."

"Then they are good. Thanks, Annie. I have a silhouette of a Welsh Terrier all ready for them to scan into their computer."

"How big a sign are you thinking about?"

"An oval, maybe a foot long, eight or ten inches high. Dark green with gold lettering, and a gold terrier in the middle. I want the look to be elegant, not affected."

"You should get stationery to match, like they have in those old movies."

"That's a great idea! I'm ridiculously excited about this, and I don't know why."

"Maybe you just want to feel like it's finally your home—yours and Nick's," Annie commented wisely.

I stared at her.

"Face it, Emma. Here at the office, you're surrounded by the McCook family. At home and in New Hampshire, it's wall-to-wall Benningtons. Even if they're not around all the time, that's pretty tough. No one would blame you for wanting your own niche."

"Thanks."

"Anytime. By the way, your next appointment is here."

I stopped by Lisa's on the way home to say hello and kiss Joy's nose.

"I can't believe how quickly the new barn has gone up, Lisa!"

"Want a tour?"

"Great."

Lisa and Jack had designed their dream barn. The stalls had big windows and were full of light and cross ventilation. The aisle was unusually wide, and rubber mats were set into the concrete to make sweeping up easier. There were six permanent stalls, plus space to create additional stalls in the equipment area. The tack room was supplied with shelves for each boarder, as well as a designated area for trunks. Saddle racks and bridle hooks were neatly arranged on the far wall. And the bathroom!

"Wow! I love the polished stone floor."

"Come and look at the office."

"Nice rug. Have you decided on a name for the farm yet?"

"We've finally agreed on Birch Creek Farm, in honor of that huge twin birch near the stream."

"I like it. How much more time to get everything completed?"

"We still need some wiring done, some carpentry and tile work in the upstairs apartment, and there's an issue with the drain in the wash stall. A few other little things. They are hoping to be done before Labor Day."

"How's Sharon doing with Olivia? I don't know a thing about Equitation."

"So far, so good. Sharon's smiling again."

"That's something."

"You have no idea. I was getting really tired of picking up the pieces every time Sharon had a miserable lesson. When we got home, it got even worse."

"I'm sure. Laura and I have talked about our fantasy of finally finding a trainer that we could feel comfortable staying with. My record so far is a year and a half."

"When Sharon was showing her pony, we were with the same teacher for six years. But since she's graduated to horses, it's been one continual nightmare. Injuries, dramas, bad advice, and the money-grubbers! And now we've built this farm. Too late to take up tennis, I suppose."

"Probably so."

"Well, I'm holding my breath about Olivia."

"I think we all are at this point."

The Civil Litigation Section of the Connecticut Bar Association was holding a special seminar on Thursday afternoon. An interesting condemnation case that had come out of the Milford Superior Court had made its way up to the Connecticut Supreme Court. A good friend of Nick's had just argued the matter for the Town of Milford in front of the United States Supreme Court. Constitutional law fascinated me. I was eager to hear discussion about cases that had been generated by the last clause of the Fifth Amendment.

Julia Newton was handing out the outline for the evening's talk.

"Emma! Haven't seen you in ages!"

We took seats on the aisle near the back door. I always like to feel that I can make a quick exit.

"… nor shall private property be taken for public use without just compensation." Attorney Eli Nelson began his comments from the podium at the front of the room. "We'll start with the basics. Eminent domain is the power by which a government asserts its authority to condemn property because it is useful to the public. Inverse condemnation cases, or confiscation claims, arise when a municipality uses its police power to restrict land development, permitting only minimal use…."

Two lawyers whom I did not recognize conducted their own discussion directly behind us.

"You hear about my big win with the Supremes last week, Al? I've been getting emails from all over the state."

"Yeah, good, Marv. How about that article on me in the *Tribune* last month? There's no question of my making partner now."

"Sure, but you'll probably need to log more time with the appellate work. I've been going up to Hartford regularly for two years."

"OK, but I do the night hearings in front of the town boards every week. You have to get in on these cases from the ground floor...."

I strained to hear the speaker. "An important question is whether to bring constitutional claims in state or federal court. With regard to takings matters, a plaintiff is required to use available state court procedures to obtain compensation. For a review of the test applied, please see *Williamson County Regional Planning Commission v. Hamilton Bank*, which was decided in 1985. The cite is 473 U.S. 172 at 195."

"Hey, Al. Did you take my advice on that adverse possession question?"

"I decided not to pursue it, Marv. My senior partner said...."

"You should have gone for it. I won a matter that was directly on point with your problem just a few months ago. I could have given you a copy of the trial memorandum that I filed. The judge basically pasted it into his opinion."

"Then I could just pull up the opinion online."

Julia turned and glared at Al and Marv. Her success was negligible.

"Pursuant to Article first, Section 11 of the Connecticut Constitution, a taking may result from a substantial interference with private property which nullifies its value, or by which the owner's right to its use is curtailed or destroyed. The specific language is as follows: 'the property of no person shall be taken for public use without just compensation therefore.' The Fifth Amendment to the U.S. Constitution applies to State government through the due process clause of the Fourteenth Amendment."

"Did you get my fax on the Groton case, Marv? You need to get the ball rolling on that discovery we asked for."

"Yeah, they're dragging their feet. I'm really tight with the town engineer—he always listens to what I say. I could give him a call …."

I stood up and faced both Neanderthals. "*Gentlemen*," I growled in a low voice, "would you *kindly* take your fascinating discussion out in the hall? You're disrupting everyone around you." There was a low chorus of agreement from the nearby members of the Bar. The bozos got up and moved to the other side of the room.

"Good job," Julia said, patting my forearm.

"Thanks. It was just their bad luck that I've had wicked PMS all week."

Attorney Nelson was still deep into his topic. "The financial effect on a particular owner must be balanced against the health, safety and welfare of the community. The test is stated in *Chevron Oil Company v. Zoning Board of Appeals of the Town of Shelton*. The cite is 170 Conn. 146 at page 151 …."

That night, I dreamed that the Christmas tree is still in the living room. It is dried and brittle, and dead needles are all around it on the floor. I'm looking at it with despair, trying to summon the energy to take the tree down. I am dirty and disheveled, and badly in need of a shower.

Then, I'm in my study, and Nick's daughter is telling me that it's her room now. Heavy torrents of water pour through the ceiling.

Finally, I'm up at the lake house in New Hampshire. There is a violent storm, and the lake water is whipping around in the high wind. My kayak is floating in front of our deck. I watch in horror through the window as the boat is swamped and sinks.

Water always symbolized emotion. I assumed that the leaks, the storm and the boat had to do with an overload of emotion. The dead tree probably represented what's left of my spirit after years of existing without nurturing or emotional support. I looked up windows in my reference books, and for once the explanations were consistent—windows framed our view of a situation.

On Saturday, Abby and I met Laura for lunch at Diane's Café on Main Street in Ridgefield. We sat down at one of the sidewalk tables, and I tied Abby's leash to my chair. The waitress very kindly brought her a bowl of water.

We ordered ham and asparagus quiche with salad, and a sausage link for Abby.

"Is Steve home this weekend?" I asked.

"No. He's in Denver for a meeting. Then he flies to Seattle on Wednesday."

"That's got to be tough."

"I don't know. He likes to travel, although he does seem to prefer to come home in between and recharge. What's strange is that when he's actually in the house, it disturbs my routine, almost as if he's a guest."

"Oh."

"Exactly." There was a pause. "What are your plans for Joy this month?"

"I'll take as many lessons as I can, but we have some big trials coming up in September, and I really need to focus."

"And you can't afford to get hurt."

"There's that. I'm very grateful for Olivia, by the way. So is everyone at Lisa's barn, so thanks again for the referral. She's the first real jumper rider that Joy has had. I could feel the difference right away. Joy is much more balanced and confident, especially to the left—which was always her more difficult side."

"The great part is that Olivia is a lovely person. No ego non-sense. None of that 'my time is more valuable than yours' attitude."

"Her lessons are actually fun. Not that Jeannie's weren't, but I come away now with a sense of accomplishing a goal. At the risk of sounding like a nosy female, do you know what Olivia's marital status is?"

"She had a pretty upsetting divorce a while back, which is why she disappeared for a few years. I think I heard Madeline say once that Olivia was living with someone in the Danbury area now, but I'm not sure about much more. Why?"

"She spends so much time in the horse world. I just don't see how anyone could have a real life beyond showing. Even police officers get days off."

"And they certainly live in the real world. No, I think with horse people that it's a passion more than a career. They're either married to other horse people—and we've seen what a disaster that can be—or they have Hollywood-like relationships and are forced to fly across country to be together. It must be very isolating. I don't know, maybe they prefer life to be that way."

"As if they're all running away from something? I've always felt that. I've learned to distance myself emotionally from horse professionals. Every time I've cared about anyone in the show world, they've turned out to be more disturbed than I can handle. I always end up backing off."

"Like Hal?" Laura asked, gently.

"Yes. I was thinking of him, specifically."

"I remember how disappointed you were when it became clear how weak a person he was."

"He was one of my closest friends, or so I thought. I had confused his amazing control and strength with horses with his character in general. There turned out to be no correlation."

"That happens in offices a good deal, too. My sister fell in love with a co-worker at her firm and was devastated when she finally realized that the man in the power suit wasn't the real person underneath, at all. It was just his work façade."

"I know a lot of men like that. I don't understand it. I'm always the same, whether I'm in court, or with my horse, or at home. Think of all the energy that is wasted on projecting that phony, impervious image."

"But you're one of the strongest people I know. Most of us aren't. We second-guess ourselves all the time. We're insecure about everything. We expect to be evaluated by what we can do as opposed to who we are, so we conjure up the persona that we imagine everyone else wants to see."

"I've never given a damn about what other people want to see. I just do my own thing."

"But that's *you*."

"I'm sorry, Laura. I can tell that you're getting frustrated with me."

"Not frustrated. Maybe a little envious. I spend a lot of time worrying about things that never come to pass, and then I get angry with myself for losing so much time on nothing. I'll bet that never happens to you."

"Well, rarely."

Laura sighed. "I wish I knew your secret. I just don't trust myself enough."

"That's the big answer, though. Being able to separate fact from bullshit. And so much of life is just pure fertilizer, you have to admit."

At that moment, Abby growled and lunged, very nearly pulling my chair with her. Her bowl flipped over, flinging water all over my feet. An enormous Great Dane strolled by with his human family. Abby leaped up, but was stopped mid-air by her leash. Laura started laughing. "Now there's another woman who refuses to be swayed by the masses! So what if the enemy is one hundred pounds heavier!"

"All she needs to be is fast enough to get her teeth in the opponent's neck. Rather like my profession, don't you think?"

"Frankly, I was thinking of the horse world. Remember what Sharon told us last year at the Hunt Club show—my best friend's broken leg means a better ribbon for me."

"Ah, yes. That, in a nutshell, is why I board my horse at a private barn."

CHAPTER SIXTEEN

Labor Day

I had a meeting with Basil Noles in the office library on Friday morning. I brought Kim in with me. This file would be a terrific learning experience for a young lawyer.

"Looks like the Armstrong trial is still going forward, Em," he announced, shoving a huge pile of deposition transcripts over to my side of the table. "Jury selection is scheduled for September fifteenth."

"How is Mrs. Armstrong doing?"

"Her doctor has put her on a very strict, supervised diet. Her husband says that she's lost almost thirty pounds."

"Good for her."

"According to the senator," Basil continued, "the weight loss has barely put a dent in the work to be done. He's worried about how the jury will react to a 'fatty.' His word, you understand, not mine."

Kim looked shocked.

"What a sensitive guy!" I remarked. "I'll bet that he has a whole flock of beautiful office assistants to remind him what an important man he is. Sorry. I know he's an old friend."

"His interns are even more attractive."

I took Kim and Annie out to lunch after the meeting had concluded.

"OK, ladies, this trial is going to be a real bear, so I'm afraid there's a lot of tedious work ahead of us in the next few weeks. Kim, your onerous task will be to summarize these depositions for me. Start with our treating physician, then their doctor. Next, do all the other fact witnesses, beginning with our clients. Annie, we're going to have to go through the medical bills and come up with a number to give the jury when they go in to deliberate. The woman didn't work outside the home, so there are no figures for lost wages."

"Are we still pressing the loss of consortium claim for the senator?" Kim asked, with disgust.

"I agree that his position is completely hypocritical. But it's our job to represent our clients and not to pass moral judgment, tempting as that may be. The jury will see through him, though, and he'll be lucky if he gets a nominal award."

"Especially if there are women on the panel," Kim added.

"We have that new client coming in this afternoon," Annie reminded us, her mouth full of cheeseburger. "The wife is in a coma as a result of childbirth, the husband has a new girlfriend, the wife's parents are suing for custody."

"Oh, my God!" Kim exclaimed.

"Don't you just love family litigation?" I grinned at her.

"Which party do we represent?"

"The father. The next few months are looking fairly grim, girls. Let's fortify with some dessert. They do great sundaes here."

There was a message on the home machine when we got in:
Hhhhiiii Dad and Emma, it's Deborah. Just calling

to see if you guys were going up to the lake for Labor
Day weekend. Because, if you are, and you have a
free room, I'd just love to bring Todd up to meet you.
Let me know! Byyyyyye."

I turned to my husband, who looked as if he was about to pull a spook and run. "Nicholas. Are we aware of a person called Todd?"

"Are *we* aware of him? No. But Deborah has told *me* that she has a new boyfriend."

"And when exactly did she do this?"

"About a month ago. When I had lunch with her. You were at the barn, I think."

Deep breaths. "OK, Nick. You know that I don't appreciate being sandbagged like this."

"You get so mad whenever I talk about her, I thought it would be better not to mention it."

"So what if I had gotten this call, Nick? She would have babbled on and on about the guy, I wouldn't have a clue, and then she'd have the pleasure of immediately getting on the phone to her mother to gleefully report that you and I don't talk and are therefore on the rocks."

"Huh?"

"Oh, never mind. Do you *want* them to come up north for Labor Day?"

"Sure. It was my idea."

"Marvelous. I need a God damn drink."

We arrived at the lake late on Thursday night. I had made a point to do the food shopping in Warwick, thus avoiding the crush of happy holiday makers in New Hampshire. I poured myself a glass of chardonnay and went downstairs to make up the basement room for Deborah and the unknown Todd.

"Why are you putting her down there?" Nick called after me.

"More privacy, that's why. They'll have the whole floor to themselves, and there's the big sitting area with TV, so they won't feel compelled to spend every waking minute with us. God willing," I said, under my breath.

"What?"

"Why don't you walk the dogs?"

"OK." I heard the screen door slam. Five minutes later, it opened again. A Long Island accent sounded from the front hall.

"Emma? It's Holly. I just saw Nick, and he said it would be all right to bother you."

"Come on down. I'm just setting up for tomorrow's guests."

Holly appeared in a Smith College sweatshirt and pink Bermuda shorts. "Jeff and I were wondering if you were free for dinner tomorrow night. We're grilling various delicacies, and I'm making a huge pasta salad. Carla will be up from school for the weekend."

"That would be great, as long as you can handle Nick's daughter and her new man. We've never met him, so no guarantees."

"Oh, it will be fine," Holly said breezily. "I get along perfectly well with Jeff's daughters and their husbands. How about five-thirty, then, and we'll go from there."

Our deck on the ground level wrapped around most of the house. We were situated on a point of land, which afforded us a water view on three sides. At ten on Friday morning, I pulled the green chaise to the side that overlooked the boat launch area. Abby hopped up and settled in against my right side, like a furry hot water bottle. I was working on my second ice tea and deeply into my novel, when the voice, that bane of my existence, floated over the clear air like smog on the Jersey Turnpike.

"Daaaaaaad! We're herrrrrrrrre!"

Was the sun over the yardarm yet? Because I could really use some hair of the dog.

Deborah and the boyfriend appeared from the other end of the deck. I got up too quickly, and poor Abby ended up in a heap on the boards.

"Emma, this is Todd," Deborah purred. He was quite nice looking, actually. Tall, semi-football build, wavy, dark blond hair, green eyes. We shook hands. Todd made a point of checking out my pink tank top. At my age, any positive appraisal was appreciated.

Nick came through from the living room, and Deborah immediately commenced her perfect daughter routine. I repaired to the kitchen and mixed myself a Bloody Mary. I heard the traffic move downstairs and returned to the deck in safety. Abby very kindly had elected to keep my seat warm in the interim. But the peace did not last.

"Emma, I've suggested that we all go down to the beach for a swim."

"Dad says that you have a new kayak, Emma."

"I told her that you'd be happy to let her take it out later." He looked at me pleadingly. Thank God we'd hit the liquor store on the drive up.

"Yes, of course," I replied, without glaring. "Let's see if we can borrow one of Holly's boats for Todd."

I had been swimming since I was two, when my parents found me paddling around in the deep end of a friend's pool and very nearly had simultaneous coronary arrests. According to my sister, my talent was due solely to natural buoyancy.

I was the first to be changed, and ran with my towel down the slope to the sandy area just a few hundred feet from our house. The water was still very warm. I used the crawl stroke until I approached the float, then flipped over on my back and executed a few three-quarter turns. I switched to the sidestroke and proceeded under the rope boundary to the middle of West Cove. As Nick and his daughter were not good swimmers, I had hoped to buy myself a little time. I had not factored Todd into the equation. He appeared at my side within moments.

"Swim team," he said, treading water.

"Oh, good."

"I'm not in your way, am I?"

"Well, the thing is, Todd, this lake covers hundreds of acres, and yet, here you are. A whole foot away. That *was* your foot, wasn't it? Not a size-twelve catfish or anything, right?"

"I just thought we made a connection back there." He flashed a big schoolboy grin. About twenty years ago, he might have gotten somewhere with me.

"So, how long have you known Deborah?"

"Spring semester. She was in my biology class."

"Biology, huh?"

"Yeah, I'm pre-med."

"I think your girlfriend is trying to get your attention."

Deborah was moving toward us in my kayak at an impressive rate of speed. The lake was definitely losing its isolated quality.

Todd frog-kicked out to meet her. I took the opportunity to power crawl in the opposite direction and got out of the water at the boat launch. Holly and her brood were established there with beach chairs and inflated alligators. In her usual indefatigable manner, Holly had assessed the situation.

"That's the guy, eh? Seems friendly."

"Yeah. I've got a real warm and fuzzy going on right now."

"Five-thirty, then?"

"Ah, yes. Cocktail hour. Absolutely."

At five o'clock, Nick pulled two bottles of chardonnay out of the wine fridge and waved them at me. "Are these OK, Em?"

"Yep. I'm sure Holly will have reinforcements, if necessary."

"Oh, Deborah wants to know what the dress code is."

"White gown and a chastity belt."

"No, help me out here, Emma."

"Jeans are fine. I'm going up to change. Have the dogs been walked?"

"The kids did the honors. Abby bit Todd on the ankle."

That night, I dreamed that I am frantically looking for my keys. I go through my purse, I check my coat pockets—nothing. I go to my desk and pull out all the drawers. In the bottom right-hand drawer I find dozens of keys on rings, plus a pair of scissors.

I couldn't find a reference to desk in any of the books, but a drawer was about something that's been kept hidden, and scissors represented control and decisiveness. A key was the symbol of the solution to a problem.

What was the key to my problem? I wasn't actually sure that I knew what the problem was. I was so dissatisfied with everything in my life, I felt like screaming all the time. But I knew that if I did, no one would understand how to help me.

Part III Verdict

A jury's finding or decision on the
factual issues of the case.

Black's Law Dictionary

CHAPTER SEVENTEEN

Assault

On Thursday night, Nick got home from the Conservation Commission meeting at eleven-thirty. I noted a big smile on his face, as he poured his single malt whiskey over the customary two ice cubes.

"Cliff got his fountain!" he announced. For a man who normally represented the owners of hospitals, shopping centers and airports, this seemed to be an unprecedented amount of glee.

"God, do I love to put one over on those simple bastards!"

"Nicholas, I'm amazed. That is a statement that is much more likely to issue from my mouth, not yours."

"Maybe you're finally rubbing off on me. The morons had no expert of their own, and no reason to discredit the reports of either of our experts. It wasn't until I reminded their counsel of the law that they backed down and gave Cliff his permit."

That night in bed, Nick surprised me by suddenly rolling over and tickling my breast. I just lay there while he pulled off my nightshirt and started kissing me. He ran his hand down my torso and pushed my legs apart. Then he was on top of me. He wrapped his arms around the pillow under my head, crushing my face into his chest. I struggled to breathe. I felt him ram his penis into me. I screamed, but he kept on going.

I called Kate from my study as soon as Nick got up to take a shower.

"I know what rape feels like," I told my sister, my teeth chattering. "He knew exactly what he was doing. He lulled me into thinking we were going to make love, and then I was screaming. And he got off on it."

"I don't know what to say, Emma. I can't believe this. What are you going to do?"

"What can I do? I can't afford to leave him."

"Did he say anything?"

"Nope. He just groaned, rolled off me, and walked into the bathroom. It was as though I wasn't even there."

"You have to talk to him. This can't happen again."

"Don't worry," I said grimly. "It won't."

Basil and I were to meet in the office library at eight the following morning to go over our strategy for jury selection on Senator Armstrong's case. Kim helped me gather together the file, the trial notebooks, and the original exhibits that were going to be submitted to the judge as evidence. Kim glanced at the photos of Mrs. Armstrong in the buff, and winced.

"The men decided to put them in, so don't blame me," I said, thinking about the night before. "That's the problem with being second seat in litigation. The ultimate decision is made by someone else."

"They said that she's lost some weight, though, right?" Kim looked hopeful. "But how will that affect the jury? Will they decide that she should have done that anyway, before her accident, so it's not the fault of the other driver that her recovery was so long?"

"Now you're thinking like a trial lawyer! They may reach that conclusion, of course. However, it is always better to mitigate damages. It would have been much more risky to have her remain obese and claim further pain."

Annie met us in the library with ice coffees and a big box of doughnuts. Basil and Mrs. Armstrong were already seated. I noted that she was drinking black tea and was eyeing a French cruller that was nearest to her on the table. Annie reached out and pushed the box closer to Kim. Mrs. Armstrong sighed and squeezed out her tea bag.

Basil started the meeting. "Now, we are going to have to pre-mark all our exhibits for I.D. with the clerk before evidence begins. Kim, I'm going to leave that to you. Please make sure that your list is complete and accurate."

Kim looked apprehensive.

"Emma, I'm going to ask you to take the direct testimony of our client and her husband, and probably our experts. I'm going to handle cross-examination of the defense's witnesses."

"Got it. Are we still sticking to the consortium claim?"

"The Senator was very specific. He will be here to testify on the first day only, I'm afraid, so if we have to interrupt Marybeth's testimony to put him on, so be it."

Basil checked his notes and stuffed half a blueberry muffin into his mouth. Mrs. Armstrong whimpered quietly.

"I've decided that we don't want to risk digital glitches, so I'm going to bring the big easel, and we'll do the computations on a large pad for the jury. Kim, your handwriting is better than mine, so I'm going to have you help me with the medical expenses, past and future. Make sure that you remind me to have it marked as an exhibit."

"OK." Kim was clearly beginning to feel the strain.

"Now that everyone has had their fill of sugar—beg your pardon, Marybeth—let's get down to jury selection questions. Annie has done an excellent job with the trial notebooks. Are there any last minute issues regarding prospective jurors before we pack up for the courthouse?"

"Any news on what opposing counsel will be like?" I asked.

"No clue. He or she will be one of about sixty lawyers that they have on staff at Posner and Underwood. Theoretically, said attorney will also try the case, but you never know."

"What about Judge Lombardi? Is he going to make one more attempt at settling?"

"No doubt in my mind. Why write a jury charge when you don't have to?"

Kim and Annie rode with me to the Superior Court in New Haven. "I've never liked this city," Annie commented, as we drove by Yale-New Haven Hospital. "The only thing it's got going for it is the university."

"And the pizza," Kim added.

"I like the shore towns just east of here, though. Clinton and Branford and Guilford. They have some very pretty areas."

"I've often thought of renting a house on the beach out there," I replied. "But Nick doesn't like the seacoast much."

"And he's got his lake," Annie said.

"Right."

According to the list on the board in the case-flow office, we were to conduct business in courtroom 3A. We unloaded our various receptacles onto the counsel table closest to the jury box.

A very tall, but heavily built man in his forties strode through the double doors. He dumped his two bags with a thud on the other table and extended his hand to Basil.

"Joe Sforzini," he informed Basil in a very strong, New York City accent. "Posner and Underwood."

"Basil Noles. This is my partner, Emma Carbury, and our associate, Kim...."

Sforzini snorted. "Any sign of the judge yet? I wanna get going on this."

"The judge will see counsel in chambers in five minutes," announced the clerk. Kim and I assembled our note-taking supplies. Basil took a copy of the complaint and answer with special defenses, and tucked them into his leather folio.

Sforzini glanced at our entourage. "All of you going in at once? Kinda like a gang bang, isn't it?"

The Honorable Bartholomew Lombardi was seated at his desk as we were escorted into his sanctum. He was a very thin man with black hair growing out of his nose and ears. He had an individual taste in ties. That morning, he was wearing a Tuscan landscape with a background in deep purples and yellows. The clerk very kindly brought in an extra chair for Kim.

Sforzini smirked. "I guess the old saying still holds, huh, Judge? The more lawyers they bring, the weaker their case."

Kim regarded him with disgust.

"And look at this sweet young thing. Barely out of law school, are you?" He leered at her chest.

Kim pulled back in alarm.

Nearly twenty years in the legal profession dropped away from me right then.

"Look, *Counselor*. Can we cut the male chauvinist bull and get straight to the numbers? Who was just whining out there about putting this show on the road?"

Basil registered terror, but the judge laughed. "I detect a specific borough in that speech, counselor. What part?"

"Bay Ridge, your honor, near the Shore Road Park."

"Fort Hamilton, myself." We grinned at each other. "Now, then, is there an offer on the table, people?"

"We aren't any closer than last time, Judge," Basil replied, regaining his poise.

"Yeah, but I noticed that the fat wife has dropped some tonnage in the meanwhile," Sforzini added. "Maybe that will change your tune?"

I twisted in my chair. "The only thing that will change my tune, *Counselor*, is taking a swing at you with an extra heavy...."

"I doubt that there is more to be said, your honor," Basil said hurriedly, adjusting his own tie. "We are probably ready to address the full panel."

"Right you are," Judge Lombardi replied as he rose from the chair and reached for his robe. "I can't wait for this trial to begin. I'm going to ask for two state marshals to be present, just in case."

Chapter Eighteen

Laura's Story

"So you have three jurors?" Laura asked later that evening at her barn. "How many do you need?"

"Six, plus two alternates."

"The other lawyer sounds like a real toad."

"Unbelievable. He had one prospective juror leave the court-room in tears, he was so crude."

"Won't the judge say anything?"

"The judge is just as bad. And he won't deign to sit in on jury selections."

"At least your partner is there to keep you from murdering anyone."

"True. The man lives in fear."

"As does your husband," Laura grinned. I didn't reply.

Laura steered me over to a table near the largest paddock. The sun was starting to set early again, which saddened me, but the view to the hills beyond the river was spectacular. I studied their purple reflection in the water.

"Emma, there's something that I need to say to you."

"I had the feeling. Is it Steve?"

"Yes, and no. It's me."

I waited.

"I know that you listen to people's crazy problems all day long, and that fact makes me feel guilty. But at the same time, it gives me hope that you'll be the one person who will understand what I'm about to say."

I didn't reply. It's usually best to just let them talk.

"Emma, I know why women shop."

This was not what I was expecting. "Why they shop?"

"Yes. Especially the women in this area. I know why they buy the designer outfits and all the jewelry and get the facials, and pedicures, and pay huge amounts for injections to beef up their lips and freeze their foreheads. I know why they join tennis clubs and do lunches out, and spend afternoons at garden club meetings. They're filling in. They're compensating for all the love and nurturing that they will never get at home. All the emptiness."

"That's probably true," I said.

"Look at us. The hours we spend at our barns, and the money we fork out, to futz around at horse shows in the heat and the rain and put our wonderful animals through hell, keeping them in vinyl stalls with no turnout. And we're spending thousands! To use latrines like we did thirty years ago at Girl Scout camp. It's insane. Well," she paused, "you don't anymore. But the rest of us do."

"No, but I understand what you mean."

"It's all a bandage. A hiding place. An escape. We poke fun at the horse professionals and how weird and dysfunctional they are. But we, the show amateurs, are just as odd, for perhaps the same reasons."

She took a deep breath.

"I married Steve fourteen years ago. At the time, I knew that he had intimacy problems. His family was never close; they were very poor, and there were drinking issues and the usual lack of money for three kids to have anything more than the basics. Then, his mom got hospitalized for alcoholism. You've heard this kind of thing over and over, I'm sure. But I made the classic mistake— I thought that I could help him. And, of course, I was wrong. I kept telling myself that if I didn't give up, I would eventually break down his barriers and get him to trust me with his feelings. But nothing was there. He's gentle, but not generous. He's not particularly bright—his success in business is the result of a good memory and hard work. I honestly don't believe that he could think his way out of a paper bag. He is oblivious to anything that doesn't directly concern himself, and he is completely unconcerned with fellow members of the human race."

"I'm sure his job hasn't helped matters."

"The distance between us has been exacerbated by his traveling for business, but that isn't the source of the rift."

"Have you reached some kind of conclusion?"

"I know that my life can not continue as it has, or *I'll* end up in the hospital. But all this is leading up to what I want to tell you. I'm having an affair."

"I see."

"You're not shocked?"

"Lord no. What's his name?"

"Reg. He's an investment broker for one of the big Manhattan firms. I met him at a seminar in Stamford."

"So, he's smart. That's good."

"And, Em, the sex is phenomenal!"

"What, if anything, have you said to Steve?"

"Nothing yet. I wanted to talk to you first."

"I'm going to send you to a friend of mine in Westport. She'll take a no-nonsense line and get you fixed up as quickly as possible."

Laura looked relieved. "Thanks so much. I know that this will be awful for everyone, but I'm ready. It's long overdue."

I sighed.

"Your turn," Laura said.

"How did you know?"

She squeezed my hand. "Your usual sparkle has been absent for months now. You're like a photocopy of yourself. Colors out of focus and fuzzy around the edges."

"That's exactly how I've felt. But I'm working on it. Something's got to break soon, or I'll lose my mind."

I drove home from the barn that day in an elevated mood, sing-ing along with Tina Turner, and visualizing Joy sailing over the big jumps with a grin on her face. I made careful turns around the reservoir and came up behind two college-age girls in an orange Jeep Wrangler. They were laughing, and the young woman in the passenger seat was fiddling with the radio. I heard Tina echoing from their speakers. A bumper sticker to the left of their license plate said "*Go with your heart, not with your fear.*"

On Sunday morning, I was pressed into having brunch with Audrey and one of her church friends, at Sandy's house in Ridgefield. We were greeted at the door by the family's huge golden retriever, name of Dave, who immediately acknowledged me as a kindred spirit. Sandy presented herself: short, blond hair, glasses too big for her face, wearing a lime green polyester dress with palm fronds waving all over it. She gave me one of those full-body once-overs, as women so often do, and led us out to the deck where she started pouring mimosas. Sandy handed me a glass.

"Emma, you're going to just *hate* me, but you've got your shirt on inside-out."

"Oh, *really*, Emma."

I felt the back of my neck. "Crisis averted, ladies. The tag was out, that's all." I finished my drink in two gulps and handed my glass back to my charming hostess.

"Another, Emma?"

"Definitely. I mean, please."

We sat down to loaded omelets and asparagus salad. Dave wandered over to my right side and placed his nose on the table, looking hopeful.

"You know a real softie right away, don't you, sweetie?" I said, scratching him behind the ears.

Sandy swiveled around in her chair and glared at me. "If you give him any food, I'll cut off your hand!"

"*Do* try not to be rude, Emma," added my mother.

"So, I hear that you have a stepdaughter," Sandy commented, spearing a large chunk of ham with her fork.

"True."

"Is she married?"

"Not yet."

"Well, it'll happen before you know it. Then the babies will start coming."

"Yes, Emma dear. No more quiet weekends at the lake for you and Nick. Of course, *I've* never been invited there, but I hear from your sister that it's lovely."

"Nick's not that wild about little kids, either, actually."

Sandy smirked. "Oh, don't be a fool. The first time he holds one of his grandchildren, it will be all over. They'll bond, and then he'll want them around all the time."

"I've always been just *destroyed* that Emma didn't want to have children of her own," chimed in Audrey. "But she's never liked them."

"Well, she shouldn't try to influence the way her husband feels about them. It's *his* family, after all."

I could feel a wall of rage rise up in my chest.

I excused myself quickly and grabbed my purse as I sprinted to the nearest restroom. I sat on the edge of the whirlpool tub and called Kate.

"Come *on*, Em!" she said, laughing. "You're so much smarter than this. Turn it around. Yank their chains a little. You know that Audrey's main button with you has always been kids. Work it!"

"Yeah, you're right. But what's with this churchy broad? Why are her knickers in a twist? I barely know her, for God's sake."

"What are you wearing?"

"Uh, my new red silk knit tank and the little beige skirt with the pocket on the hem."

"Legs nice and tan?"

"Sure. Whatever. What's your point, Kate?"

"You've got that fabulous hourglass figure. That's the point. Women hate you on contact. It's happened all your life. Why don't you get that?"

"This female is in her sixties! Does she think I want to steal her husband?"

"No. She's just jealous. Like I used to be."

"You never told me that."

"It's true. Then my boobs got bigger after I had Hannah. Now I look like a scaled-down model of you, which makes me happier."

"Oh, good."

"Now, get out there and act like a professional strategist instead of a seventh grader."

Little sisters can occasionally be very helpful people.

Audrey was into her fifth mimosa and still going strong.

"Well, yes," she drawled, waving her champagne flute in the air. "I was just saying to my dear sister-in-law last night how *envious* I am of her large family. I do *so* wish that Kate would have another baby. I've completely given up on Emma, of course."

"Perhaps your ship has come in, Mother," I replied, ever so sweetly. "Nick and I have been discussing the concept of adoption."

"Another *dog*, dear?"

"No, Mother. A little African American baby. Or perhaps Chinese. How does Kashequa Bennington sound?"

Audrey's eyes bulged. Her glass tipped over into her lap.

"Or maybe Chow-Lin Carbury-Bennington? Just think, Mother. You could take her to your Junior League meetings! Introduce her as your newest granddaughter!"

Portrait of an elitist snob having a seizure.

"Now you've got it!" Kate snickered, two hours later. "She must have called me the second you dropped her off at her house. I could hear the bubbly foaming in her nose."

I was still laughing. "I haven't had this much fun since Audrey had Dad cancel all their credit cards because she thought she'd left her purse at the train station!"

"And it was sitting on the family room TV the whole time!"

"Then, she shrieked at him for hours because he didn't see it." I paused. "Listen Kate, I can't do this any more."

"What?"

"Play act at being a daughter. I can't stand the woman. Her behavior is appalling. She's never been emotionally supportive of either of us, and she didn't even bother to protect me from that crazy female today. Audrey's completely up her own butt, and is incapable of any level of understanding or compassion. I've decided to cut her out of my life."

"I hear what you're saying, and my first reaction is envy. I wish I could do the same, but I have a child. Hannah should have a relationship with her grandmother."

"Well, look at it this way. Once Hannah is eighteen, she's an adult, and you're off the hook."

"Something to look forward to. Thanks."

CHAPTER NINETEEN

Murder

Judge Lombardi was wearing a particularly repellant tie: topless buxom females with yellow hair against a watermelon background. Political correctness was clearly not a concern.

Marybeth Armstrong was sworn in by the clerk. After about five minutes of background questions, I asked about the accident.

"Would you describe for the jury the effect that the impact had upon your person, if any?"

"I was thrown forward at first, but my seat belt kept me from slamming into the passenger side seat. Then, when the second car hit us from the side, I was wrenched into the door at my right."

"Did you sustain any injuries as a result?"

"Yes. There was damage to my spine, as well as very painful bruising to my chest and shoulder."

I walked over to the witness stand. "Would you please look at this photograph, Mrs. Armstrong, and tell the jury what it is?"

"It's a picture that was taken of me in the hospital the day of the accident. It shows the bruising that I've just described."

"Who was the photographer?"

"My husband, Senator William Armstrong."

"Thank you. I'll offer it."

"Any objection?" inquired his honor, of Sforzini.

"No Judge."

"Plaintiff's one."

I handed the photo to the clerk who crossed out the ID marking on the yellow exhibit sticker. He then passed it up to the judge.

There was a moment of silence. Then, the judge angled himself toward the jury box, picked up his tie, and held the picture, face-out, next to it.

"Look, ladies and gentlemen," he said gleefully. "These broads look exactly the same!"

Basil stood up, requested that the jury be excused, and then moved for a mistrial.

"Did you order a transcript?" Denise asked me, aghast, hours later.

"Yes, of course, but the whole tie thing will be lost with just dialogue."

"You should go straight to Judicial Review with this."

"I don't know. Basil can work that out with the Armstrongs, but I'm inclined to just get another judge and try to settle this case. I'm tired of it."

"You *look* tired."

"Thanks. Well, at least it was an interesting learning experience for Kim."

Denise laughed. "Between those two men, she'll be turned off to the legal profession forever."

"Don't forget David McCook, back at the office. That makes three leering lawyers. Not to mention the Senator, who took that ridiculous picture of his wife in the first place."

The Westport/Warwick Bar Association met the next night at Oscar's Seafood Restaurant in Warwick Center. I stood with Nick as our panting colleagues lined up for drinks.

The speaker for the evening, Attorney Bruce Foster, edged over to me and slung an arm around my shoulder. An aura of bourbon hit me in the face.

"So how goes it, beautiful? Any cases whipping your cream these days?"

I smothered an instant reaction of nausea and attempted to signal Nick, who was studying single malt labels with the bartender.

"Wanna take up labor litigation? I've got a spot for you, babes."

"Tempting. But not interested."

"You're the one who's tempting," he breathed in my ear, his scrawny bald head pressed into my cheek.

"Gee, thanks."

"Isn't this great? We can have dinner and spend some time together!"

Then he got right behind me and ran his hands up and down both sides of my torso. I was carrying a plate of appetizers and a glass of wine, and could do nothing.

"Are you OK?" Maria McCormack asked, as Bruce staggered over to the podium. "That guy is such a slimeball. He pulls something like this at every meeting. And he was suspended from the practice two years ago for problems with his trustee account."

"Why doesn't anyone go after him?" I asked, shaking.

"You know how people are, Emma! No balls!"

"I think I just grew a set. Statewide Grievance and I are about to get acquainted."

"Good for you."

"How about another glass of wine?"

"Sure."

"Do you want to leave?"

"I wouldn't give the creep the satisfaction. But I think I'll put my coat back on, just in case."

I called Laura at work the next morning.

"God, Emma, how disgusting. I'm so sorry."

"For the last few hours, the thought of any man touching me is so repellent that it almost makes me gag. And all I got was a grope!"

"Sounds like he copped a pretty good feel, though."

"Oh, definitely. I was wearing a dress, not a suit—one less protective layer. So, multiply my repugnance by one million and that's how rape victims react."

"Consider the incest cases. Usually the creep is someone that the victim loves, and it happens in their own homes."

"Another million. The positive side of this is that I will be a better lawyer from now on. More sensitive, anyway. I've already sent a formal complaint to Statewide Grievance. I feel like I've hit back at my Dad, my dear husband, and that creepy Bruce with one aggressive wallop."

"Good for you."

"God, Laura, I'm wondering if this was such a good idea after all."

"What do you mean?"

"I thought that returning to civil litigation would be the answer to my problems. But look at what's happened so far! I can't stomach the legal community, and after the Armstrong case, I feel like the trial process is a total farce. What the hell is going on?"

"They say that the Universe will continue to close doors, until you find the right one. Maybe this means that you're supposed to be looking in another direction. Didn't you tell me that you have really enjoyed working on the few mediation cases that you've done?"

"Yes. I've mediated a couple of divorces, a marriage, and one landlord tenant dispute." I laughed. "I really loved that I could help these people, without dealing with some money grubbing steam roller on the other side. It's very freeing. I'm sure it's the new wave for the legal profession; the old litigation model doesn't work. OK Laura, you're right. I'm going to get on this."

"Just take care of yourself. You're probably going to feel odd for a while."

"I know. Thanks."

"Where was Nick when this happened? Couldn't he stop this jerk?"

"He was over by the bar, discussing Ivy League sports with a crowd of good ole boys. He didn't even see it happen."

"And when you told him?"

"He shrugged it off. He didn't understand what the problem was."

"Oh."

"Exactly. By the way, I don't want to invade your personal space, but I am thinking about you. Always."

"Likewise. We'll have dinner soon. Life is definitely on the upswing."

"Aha. I'm looking forward already."

The McCooks weren't interested in expanding the practice to include mediation.

"I'm sorry Emma," Mr. McCook said, at the next partnership meeting. "We've talked about it, but a mediation department isn't in our foreseeable future."

"We just don't see it as a money maker," Basil added. "We count on the billable hours from court work. You know what the overhead for this office is, especially with the new associates."

"I never got the hand holding stuff anyway," David smirked. "What's fun about settling cases?"

"I thought you wanted to do civil trials, Em," Ed added. "I've got plenty of divorce work piled up, if you want to come back to family. My son is on board full time, remember, so we'll have more help."

"I'm afraid those are your options, Emma," Mr. McCook said, with finality. "We appreciate that you may decide that you want to explore other avenues."

I reported the results of the meeting over dinner at the Warwick Grill that night. Pete and Jane had joined us.

"Why don't you just open your own practice?" Pete asked. "Then you can do whatever you want."

Nick shook his head. "It would take years for her to build up a client base, and how would she pay for her office expenses in the meantime? She'd need furniture, equipment, legal liability insurance. All that costs money."

"I thought that I'd get a business loan," I replied, my voice shaking. I felt miserable. Jane looked at me with concern.

"No way that you'd get one without some collateral," Nick said, draining his martini. "And you don't have any."

"I was going to suggest that we do some estate planning, so that I actually have some assets in my name, after ten years of marriage," I began.

"This sounds like a conversation that the two of you should have at home," Jane said quickly.

The waiter came with the check, and handed it to Pete. Pete squinted in the poor light, and passed it to me, with his credit card. "You have the best eyes here, Em. Figure out what we owe. We'll split the tarif, OK buddy?" He said to Nick.

"Sure." Nick pulled out his wallet and selected a Visa. I put my hand out for it.

Nick swung his card in the air in the other direction, and grabbed the bill from my hand.

The ride home was in dead silence. I couldn't decide what had dumbfounded me more, Nick's oblivion to my frustration with my career, or the fact that he had just treated me like a five year old in front of his friends. Jane had whispered, "We'll talk," to me, as we put on our coats, but I could barely nod in reply.

We walked the terriers, and then Nick picked up the television remote.

"You can't be serious," I said. "I want to talk about the financial situation."

"What about it?" he muttered, as he scanned the TV section of the paper.

"How about the fact that after ten years of marriage, I have only a horse and half of two dogs to show for it? Even my car is leased, and you're the primary lessee. How do you think I feel, at my age, to be in a position like this?"

"It wouldn't occur to me to think about how anyone feels, Emma," he replied coldly, walking over to the couch. "What do you want me to do? Sign this house over to you? I built it twenty years before I even met you. I had the lake house twelve years before we got married. Do you think that you're entitled to part of either of them?"

"I know that I'm entitled, by law, to my fair share of the marital estate," I stammered, suddenly regretting the three glasses of wine that I drank at dinner.

Nick sat down, aimed the remote, and adjusted the channel. "Don't forget what it costs to have you here. Joy is not inexpensive. And you contribute nothing to the household."

I felt as though I'd been hit by a bus. There could be no possible response to a husband who could devalue his wife to this extent. I took Abby in my arms, went upstairs, and moved my personal items into the largest guest room.

The following afternoon Stone Meadow Road was jammed with police cars and media trucks. I edged slowly around the masses into our driveway, determined to be supportive of Cliff. What now?

I located Annette in front of a Channel 3 camera. She was cradling her darling Pepe with one arm, and gesticulating toward Cliff's new garden with the other. I followed the journalist's gaze and froze. The police had roped off the entire area, and a gurney with a body bag was being rolled toward the back of the house.

A CNN reporter shoved a microphone in my face.

"Attorney Carbury, isn't it? You're a neighbor of Clifford Wells. Did you know the deceased woman?"

I fought down the urge to start screaming. "WHO is dead?"

The man didn't bat an eye. "Wells' girlfriend. Camille Bender. He stabbed her and planted her in his garden. Some dog dug her up, and the owner called the police." He pointed to Annette. "Did you know Ms. Bender?"

My stomach heaved and a loud ringing sounded in my head. I stumbled back down our driveway and leaned on my car, breathing hard. Oh God, oh God.

I pulled my BlackBerry out of my bag and speed dialed Nick's cell. Voice mail. I got my sister in her car.

"Kate! Camille. He killed her! She's dead!" I panted.

"The Brit across the street? You sound horrible. Do you want me to come over?"

"The road is blocked to non-residents." I couldn't control my breathing. "I have to get through to Nick, but he's not picking up."

"I'll try him. Go inside and lie down. Keep the phone by you."

I managed to pull my car into the garage. I had little control of my hands, but I finally got the back door open. I could hear frenzied barking from the front of the house. I climbed the stairs to my study and curled up on my chaise.

Kate called back. "His secretary says that he's in court. I told her that there was an emergency and to call you at home. How are you doing?"

"Not good. I can't stop shaking."

"Stay warm and drink something. I'm sure that Nick will call soon." She paused. "Have the police talked to you yet?"

"No. But it's only a matter of time. That's why I want Nick to be here to deal with them." My teeth chattered. "I don't think that I can."

Ten minutes later the back door slammed. "Emma! I've got to get out there to talk to the detectives. Are you upstairs?" I heard the terriers gallop into the family room. "I'm taking Mac. Call Abby, will you?"

Abby jumped onto my stomach, licked my face, and settled down across my legs.

My thoughts went round and round like a hamster on a wheel. How can something like this happen? How can a smart, talented and beautiful woman end up in a perennial bed? Why was she engaged to a monster? Why didn't she feel threatened? They spent so much time together, and she didn't see what he was. She refused to see what he was. He seemed like such a gentleman. So much charm. His wife saw through him. She tried to warn Camille. I warned Camille that she should listen to his wife. She didn't listen, and now she's dead. Dug up by a spoiled lap dog and dead. She didn't see the danger and now it's too late. Just like *Gaslight*. But Paula got help. Poor Camille. Poor fragile, vulnerable Camille. Oh God. Oh my God! How can something like this happen?

The drumming in my head was building. It got so loud that I cried out in pain. Abby leaped up and put her face right up against mine. My heart was pounding, and the back of the chaise started thudding against the wall.

My BlackBerry played *Ode to Joy*. Laura.

"I just heard the news, Em. Are you OK?"

"No," I stammered. "I think I'm having an anxiety attack. I can't seem to move, and my breathing is totally out of control."

"I'm not surprised. Your neighbor is a killer. Probably twice over. But you're safe now. Is Nick there?"

"He's talking to the police."

"Is there anything I can do for you? What would help?"

"I don't know!"

"You know you're safe, though. Right? This is a fear reaction."

"Is it? Fear of what? Do I imagine that Cliff is going to break out of jail and use me to mulch the tomatoes?"

"You're in shock. Why don't you crawl into bed and wait for Nick to get back. Maybe have some tea."

"OK," I chattered.

"I'll call again later."

It was nearly two hours before I heard Nick come in again. He filled Mac's water bowl and went out to his study. I wrapped a comforter around me and followed him. He looked up from his desk when I came in.

"Cliff's being held at the Warwick Police Station. I've got to get down there."

"Why you? You're not a criminal lawyer."

He looked annoyed. "They're sending some big shot trial attorney from the city, but I volunteered to hold the fort until he arrives. I sat on the criminal bench for six months, remember."

I felt closed over and paralyzed. My legs began to shake. "Nick, I'm not feeling well. What about sending someone else from your firm, and staying here with me?"

He didn't even miss a beat. "Can't Em. I'm leaving directly from there to the New Hampshire house. My daughter is coming up for a long weekend. She's bringing a new boyfriend."

I dropped into the arm chair near the door. My breathing time had doubled. "I didn't know you had planned this. Please postpone it a day? I think I'm having an anxiety attack."

He began packing some files in his briefcase. "I don't want to do that. Why don't you call your sister?"

I started to plead. "Could I come up with you then? I'm afraid to stay here alone. So close to everything."

He looked up, his eyes cold. "No. That wouldn't be right. It would change the whole tone of the trip. I have to go. I'm sure your sister can handle this."

Then he was gone, leaving me with both dogs, and the pounding in my chest that felt like a heart attack.

When Kate called a half hour later, I was still curled up on the chair in Nick's study.

"God Emma, I can't believe that he just left you like that!"

I started to sob. "This marriage is a sham, Kate. It's over! I'll be destitute! Oh Christ, I'm going to lose everything and have to move in with Audrey. All that abuse again! I can't stand it. I can't even bear thinking about it. I'm losing my mind! I'm going to end up in the hospital like crazy Aunt Jocelyn!"

"You're going to put ME in the hospital if you keep this up! Don't worry, you're not going to move in with Audrey." She paused. "Besides, if you don't have any money, she won't let you."

I laughed, and suddenly felt ridiculous. I got out of the chair and started folding the comforter with one hand, my BlackBerry tucked between my ear and my shoulder.

"You know what? You're right. I'm a lawyer, dammit. A god damn good one. And I know the law. That jerk can't kick me out of here. I'll go when I'm good and ready. It's time to make some changes."

"Good for you. While you're doing that, I'm going to pour myself a very large glass of vodka. Moving in with Audrey! Don't *scare* me like that again."

CHAPTER TWENTY

Cutting the Cord

I arranged with Marilyn to meet her the next morning for an emergency Reiki session.

"Are you sure that you're ready to cut the energetic cord with your husband?" She asked. "I know that this is a big step for you."

"I'm definitely ready." I hopped on her table, which was made up like a single bed. "I finally feel clear on everything. The man is toxic and I want to be free of the emotional hooks that he's had in my life."

Marilyn grinned. "You've gotten through this so quickly, it's amazing. I've decided that you are the Poster Client for Reiki and Aromatherapy."

She dimmed the lights and turned up the classical music in the background. I lay down and pulled the blanket up to my chin, leaving my arms out and down along my sides. Marilyn took her place on the stool behind my head. She placed the small purple pillow over my eyes, and put her hands under my head. I began to relax.

"Now, Emma, I want you to take a nice, deep breath in through the soles of your feet, and slowly release it through the top of your head, clearing out any negativity that may be lingering. Good. Now take another deep breath through your feet. See the breath as a beautiful white energy, cleansing as it travels up your spine, and then release it through the top of your head. Excellent.

"You are at the gate of your special garden. Open the gate and begin to walk along the path, touching the bark of the trees, admiring the flowers, smelling the lavender, the roses. You can hear the sea below you. When you are ready, walk down your wooden staircase, until you reach the beach. I want you to feel the sun and the sand, hear the seagulls, smell the salt water, breathe with the rhythm of the waves. You stand where the warm water is just covering your toes. You are at peace.

"You see three people in the distance, and they are walking toward you. You turn toward them. They are Nick and his two children, Douglas and Deborah. You see a silver cord attached to Nick, and the other end is attached to you at the solar plexus, just above your navel. When you are ready, tell him, with compassion, what you have decided. Raise your hand when you are done."

I looked at Nick. His gray eyes looked back at me, and I could feel nothing. I saw him brush his brown hair back on his forehead, as he always did when he was nervous. He seemed resigned. I told him that my intention was to release myself from him and our marriage. I wished him the best.

I raised my right hand slightly.

"Perfect." Marilyn continued, "now visualize the silver cord between you start to dissolve. When it is gone, Nick and his children will walk away from you. Turn back to the sea.

"Now you have climbed the wooden stairs and are back in your garden of serenity. You see a comfortable bench. You sit there, feeling grounded with the earth. Suddenly your garden is ablaze with color. Flowers, fruits, birds. There is abundance everywhere you look. You feel that there will be abundance in all aspects of your life. You feel safe."

Marilyn moved away from my head and around the entire table. Wherever she placed her hands I felt warmth and relaxation. About twenty minutes later, she brought me back, with more breathing. I stretched my arms and sat up, handing her the eye pillow.

"You went really deep," she remarked. "I could see colors around you. Gold and green. You definitely did some healing today. How do you feel?"

"Calm," I replied. "Empowered. I know now that I will be fine on my own, and I'm not afraid to take the necessary steps. I'm starting to formulate an exit plan."

"You know that the more you visualize your plan, the faster it will manifest. Consider putting up a Life Board somewhere in your house. Use pictures, words from magazines, or whatever you need to make your ideas materialize. You can always make changes, and remember, be careful what you ask for, because you *will* get it."

Nick was grilling himself a steak when I got in Monday evening. Macduff suddenly picked up his head and took off for the living room, barking frantically. We followed. Fluttering around by the French windows was a large catbird. Mac jumped up on the couch and tried to fling himself at the intruder.

"Grab him!" I yelled at Nick. I ran to the front hall and opened the big door. The catbird summoned its courage and flew toward me, passed the door, and entered the dining room where it was deflected by the chandelier over the table. It perched on the sideboard, breathing hard.

"I put Mac out on the porch," Nick said. "Try waving your arms at it. I'll keep it from going back into the living room."

I flapped at the poor creature who took off with a frightened warble, banged into Nick's shoulder, and careened out the door and into the front yard. Nick turned the brass key. "How many times has this happened now?" he asked.

"This is the third," I said, as I collected wet paper towels to deal with the droppings.

"I've never seen anything like it," he said. "Not in all the years that I've owned this house."

"Maybe someone is trying to tell you something."

My painting class resumed the following week. I pulled out the landscape that I had worked on in August: a full sheet snow scene with birches and vivid blue shadows across the lake. The others gathered around as Pam offered some suggestions.

"That tree in the back looks like it's floating. See if you can't lift some of the ground color and settle it down. I like the deep greens of the pines over here. And the intensity of the contrasts. This painting really is quite well done, Emma. You should consider entering it in a show."

"Really? Where? Is one coming up?"

"The Connecticut Watercolor Society fall exhibition is next month. You'd have to drop your painting off with them around the fifteenth, and then wait to hear if the jury accepts it."

"Good grief. All right, if you think I should, Pam."

"Let's get you going on the few corrections that I want you to make, and then you can take the painting to be framed."

I had lunch with Denise on Friday.

Denise leaned forward. "Em, I've been thinking about opening my own practice, and I want you to consider coming on board. Now that we're both trained in mediation, I want to jump-start to a whole new career."

"I'm interested."

"Good. I realize that you have a lot going on. So maybe the timing isn't perfect."

"Frankly, it's the answer to a prayer. I feel as though I'm surrounded by duplicitous jerks, and I'm tired. If Nick has to pay me alimony, then so be it. I have a right to be happy."

"It's good to hear you say that. We've all been so concerned." Denise paused. "What about the name of the firm? By order of admission to the Bar, maybe?"

"Carbury and Frederickson. I like it. What about location? I'm looking at house rentals in Fairfield and Westport. Something on the water would be wonderful. The drive to see Joy will be longer, but I'll be able to use my kayak."

"I've been thinking about the Post Road in Fairfield, or even Southport. But we can talk logistics later. Let's just get through the holidays in one piece. God, I hate this time of year."

Annie surprised me with a plate of French pastries for breakfast at the office the next morning.

"What's this in honor of?" My mouth full of Napoleon. "I don't do the raises, you know."

"Not me. Remember the ghost client? He dropped by with a big box of goodies for everyone."

"Is everything OK over there? Patty isn't pulling something new, is she?"

"Not that I've heard. Mr. Ambrose just said that he'd like you to call him at your earliest possible convenience."

I went back into my office. "John? What's up? Everyone behaving?"

"Emma! Yes, all is well, thanks. I stopped by to invite you and Annie to a gathering that I'm having on Friday night. Cocktails and buffet dinner."

"Sounds great, I'll ask. What's the occasion?"

"I spent all summer completely redoing the old house, and now I want to show it off. And I've met someone."

"Definitely cause for celebration, then. I'll get back to you tomorrow, if that's all right."

"Fine. I remember how much you like real French champagne."

I left the office early to run to Norwalk and pick up my framed snowy masterpiece. I had ordered stickers for the backs of my paintings.

"They look so professional!" I said to the nice man behind the counter. I wrote "Shadows on Pequot Lake" on the first one, and the price: six hundred dollars. I would drop the painting at the Connecticut Watercolor Society gallery the next morning, for the jury to make a decision.

Olivia had built a jumper course in the ring for our lesson. Joy and I watched as she indicated the path that she wanted us to take.

"You're going to do this first line in a nice easy five strides. Remember to really stretch out your arms over the oxer; Joy likes lots of head room. Get your lead change in the corner, do the diagonal line, then roll back with the skinny to the little combination. Finish with a courtesy circle. Trust her over the jumps, and just steer. Stay balanced, get her back if she lengthens, but do it politely. Nice and slow, OK, Em?"

We were cantering our first real course! Lisa and Sharon stood by the gate to watch.

"Good release over the oxer!" Olivia shouted, as we sailed down the diagonal line, my eyes already on the roll back.

We completed the final circle, as our audience hooted enthusiastically.

Olivia was smiling. "You're both definitely ready for my Halloween gymkhana. Congratulations! You can do the Egg and Spoon, Simon Says, Bobbing for Apples, Red-light, Green-light," she paused. "Well, maybe not Red-light, Green-light. I'm not sure how Joy would feel about stopping once the buzzer goes off."

I patted Joy's neck. "Thanks, Olivia. We've come a long way, but we're finally having fun together."

"Be thinking about Joy's outfit for the costume contest," Sharon reminded me.

"I have been," I replied. "An Irish theme seems appropriate."

Annie and I arrived at John Ambrose's house in Darien at 7:15. The old farmhouse, previously a dull brown, had been stained a cozy weathered gray, with white trim and a deep green door. There were colonial brass light fixtures around both sides of the door, and beautiful arrangements of chrysanthemums and ornamental kale on the porch.

"Notice the new wallpaper," Annie whispered. The dated, prissy stuff was gone and had been replaced by elegant patterns in red and blue and gold.

John emerged from the living room, a flute of champagne in each hand. He offered one to Annie and the other to me.

"For two lovely ladies who went against their saner judgment and helped me out of a very tight jam."

"The house looks amazing," Annie said.

"A wonderful transformation," I agreed.

"May I show you around? We'll end up by the buffet, I promise."

We proceeded upstairs. I could tell that Annie was slightly apprehensive about a sequel to our previous experience. I decided to stay just out of clutching distance. We toured Charlotte's room first, which was done in a very sweet pony motif. The walls were papered to resemble pastures with white fencing, and in one corner was a turnout shed.

"I feel as though I'm on a farm in Virginia."

"Charlotte is already horse crazy. I hope I've got a few more years before I have to start shopping for a show pony. We haven't touched Tucker's room, as it had just been done," John said, "so we'll move to the master bedroom."

"Oh, good," Annie breathed.

"Here's the linen closet. Quite old-fashioned, but I love the built-in labels on the shelves. This is the last bedroom; I use it as a study. As you see, I have a view to the Sound from my desk."

I moved closer to admire and walked right through a cold patch. Uh, oh. I glanced at Annie. No reaction.

"Let's go down the back staircase this time. I want you to see the clothes press that I've just gotten for the landing."

There were about ten guests enthusiastically milling about the dining room table. I picked up a plate and set my sights on the tenderloin at the far end. Annie came up behind me.

"Feel anything yet?" She asked in a low tone.

"Just once, in the study. Have you?"

"I'm too busy adding up what all this work must have cost. Did you see the fabrics in the living room? And how about the marble double bath and the new state-of-the-art kitchen? What does this guy do?"

"Mergers and acquisitions. Very high-end and very complicated. The house is just wonderful," I said, a little wistful. "John has been through hell, and now he has his dream house, his kids are back, and look at his gorgeous new woman! I'm glad for him."

"I guess I am, too," Annie said, slightly sour. "Yes, of course I am."

John produced our coats from the hall closet at just after ten.

As he helped me with mine, he slipped a small box into my hand. "Open it when you get home," he said quietly.

I followed Annie outside. I turned to wave goodbye to John. Standing next to him was a tall elderly lady in a long dark dress. Her grey hair was pulled tightly from her face. They both waved, and just as I was about to turn back, she vanished. John smiled and closed the door.

When I got home, I hurried up to my study alone to open John's gift. Inside the little black velvet box was a magnificent brooch. It was set with garnets, pearls and small diamonds in swirls of gold filigree. On the back was engraved the initials ECA. Elizabeth Conway Ambrose. The brooch was a present from John's grandmother.

The next morning, I got out of the shower and reached for my watch. It was a reproduction of a 1930s Hamilton that I'd had for years. Many wristbands and batteries later, it had never let me down, until now. The second hand was still. The clock had stopped just after midnight.

I put it in my purse and added "jewelers" to my list of errands for the day.

That afternoon, I was looking for copies of our latest tax return to fill out a new credit card application. I went through my file cabinet and the desk drawers in my study, but no luck. Nick was in Stamford playing hockey. I walked through the breezeway and out to his office. I knew that the files from the accountant were kept in the bottom right-hand side of his desk.

I pulled out the heavy folder, located the tax return, and made notes of last year's figures. I bent to replace it, and my eye caught the label of an accordion file still in the drawer. It was labeled New Will; Revised Life Insurance Policies.

I began reading and my jaw dropped. Nick had completely disinherited me from all the marital assets, in favor of his kids. He had also changed the beneficiaries on the policies. The revisions were all dated over a year ago.

"Oh my God, Em!" Kate was horrified. "What are you going to do?"

"I'm going to nail the bastard to the wall."

"I don't get it. What was going on two summers ago? Why would Nick do this to you?"

"I've been thinking about that. This may be retaliation for spending so much time at the barn with Hal, who was never more than a good friend. Or it might be about the big blowout we had when Deborah wanted to move into the New Hampshire house for the summer."

"And you said no. I remember that fight."

"Nick has always been a big baby when it comes to emotional issues. He has rages like a three-year-old and makes stupid decisions. Then suddenly his feathers are smooth, as though nothing had ever happened."

"But he didn't fix this. What if he had died?"

"I would have spent years in litigation against his kids, with only my salary to live on. Enough. At least I'm cured of any guilt that I may have been feeling about leaving. Nick is about to find out just how good a lawyer I am." I clenched my fists. "And I'm sure as hell not waiting until January to find a new home. I'm long overdue for a place of my own."

When Nick drove up later that afternoon, I was sitting in the family room with Macduff and Abby. I heard him open the door to his study, and then the almost immediate slam as he charged through the garage and banged into the back hall.

I had left the file open on his desk. He came in, waving it, papers skidding across the floor.

"You were in my desk drawer," he snorted, stating the obvious.

"I've already made copies," I reported calmly, "and I've placed them in my safe deposit box in town. Denise will find the faxed copies in her office Monday morning."

"What do you mean?"

I stood up. "What do YOU mean? What gives you the right to disinherit me from my own money? Do you realize that if you had died suddenly, I would have been practically penniless, with just my income, and no where to live?"

"I thought about it." His face was a frozen mask.

"You THOUGHT about it? You didn't even leave me any life insurance!"

"Where would you have gone if you hadn't come here?" He sneered. "To your mother's? I took you in. You were just a court clerk. You were lucky to be here. All my hard work. It *should* go to my kids." The veneer of charm and civility had disappeared completely. His lack of concern for me was so cold that it was terrifying. "The arrangement was fine while you did your job for me. But then you bought your horse, and everything was about her." His eyes turned black. "You'll have real trouble keeping her now."

Suddenly I realized that he had been aware of what he was doing to me all along; taking advantage of my fear of the past repeating itself, and intentionally creating anxiety about Joy, from the beginning. All of the feelings of unbalance and vulnerability, all of the dreams, and here was the cause. I steadied my breathing as Marilyn had taught me.

"The *arrangement*? This is a *marriage*, Nicholas, and as your wife, I am protected by Connecticut law. The State places a value on my contribution to this marriage, even if you never did. I'll have Denise serve you with a divorce summons and complaint as soon as possible." I laughed. "A little professional advice. Don't make any other unilateral changes from now on. Family judges are ferocious when defendants play games with marital assets."

He glared and stomped out. Mac put his front paws up on my knees and gave me a look of concern. I picked him up.

"Don't worry Sweetie," I said, kissing his nose. "I'll always be your mom."

"This has been one hell of a year, hasn't it?" Kate remarked. We were sitting on a bench at Hannah's school, watching Hannah's team at soccer practice.

"And next year promises to be equally as interesting," I added. "A marshal served Nick with my divorce complaint on Tuesday morning, right in front of his partners at work. He's going to fight, so mediation is out of the question. Denise told me that she has rarely seen a financial picture that is so disparate in terms of distribution of assets."

"I'm not surprised. He kept you on such a tight financial leash all those years. He was literally banking on the fact that you wouldn't rock the boat. You were supposed to be so grateful for your nice life." Kate turned to watch as Hannah got the ball away from the other team, and passed it to a teammate. "Em, I want to apologize to you. I should have been more compassionate when you tried to tell me what was going on with you last Christmas. I was dealing with my own issues, and dumping them on you, which was totally unfair. The truth is, I really want to have another baby, but the thought of Audrey's abuse if I quit my job, or take a pay cut! It seems ridiculous now. I trust Tom."

"Why don't you two make a post marital agreement? Something so that you feel more secure? It will be your choice whether or not to share the information with Audrey. And really, why should you?" My voice sounded a little bitter.

Kate squeezed my arm.

"Do you honestly think that Nick has that personality disorder you were talking about?"

"Narcissistic Personality Disorder? Probably. He's a perfect match, according to the information that I've found on the internet, and from the seminar materials. Phony charm, faked intimacy, duplicity, unhealthy self importance, control, devaluing of the partner, systematic chipping away of the partner's self esteem. It explains why I always felt like I was on the deck of a sinking ship. I could never find solid footing in the marriage. The really funny thing is that I was the problem solver in the house. The man couldn't change a light bulb without consulting me. And he was hopeless with anything to do with electronics."

"As well as with his kids."

"Audrey is also a perfect match for NPD, by the way, which if true, makes her a rarity. The statistics show that at least 75% of these people are men. No wonder Dad drank himself to death."

"I've never been swayed by stats. The numbers assume too much. What's really impressive to me is that having escaped Audrey's clutches, you ended up in the fire with a real Master of the Universe."

I grinned. "According to my research, people will continue to play out the same behavior patterns over and over, until they acknowledge the wounding from their childhoods, and take steps to heal. It explains why my dreams were so confused; half had to do with our delightful upbringing, the other to do with my marriages." I sighed.

"What? Are you worried about the divorce?"

"No. Actually, I was thinking about Camille. I warned her, you know. Not long before she was killed. Cliff's wife had really laid into her about him."

"What did you tell her?"

"That wives always know. They can live in denial, and very often do. I did. But in the final analysis, my female clients would consistently tell me the same thing. They were just too paralyzed with fear for their futures to commit to action." I paused to clap, as Hannah made a goal. "But as far as I'm concerned, that ends now."

The night after Halloween, I had a dream. Abby, who has grown to the size of a Great Dane, is chasing Deborah down Warwick's Main Street.

Very gratifying.

Recommended Reading

Sylvia Browne's Book of Dreams by Sylvia Browne with Lindsay Harrison, Penguin Group (USA) Inc. (2003).

The Complete Dream Book by Gillian Holloway, Ph.D., Sourcebooks, Inc. (2001).

The Hidden Meaning of Dreams by Craig Hamilton-Parker, Sterling Publishing Co. Inc. (1999).

The Everything Dreams Book by Jenni Kosarin, F+W Publications, Inc. (1988, 2005).

Reiki Energy Medicine: Bringing Healing Touch into Home, Hospital, and Hospice by Libby Barnett and Maggie Chambers, Healing Arts Press (1996).

Aromatherapy for the Soul by Valerie Ann Worwood, New World Library (2006).

Betrayal of Innocence, Incest and its Devastation by Dr. Susan Forward and Craig Buck, Penguin Group (USA) Inc. (1978, 1988).

Secret Survivors, Uncovering Incest and its Aftereffects in Women by E. Sue Bloom, Ballantine Books (1990).

Father-Daughter Incest by Judith Lewis Herman, Harvard University Press (1981, 2000).

Trauma and Recovery by Judith Herman, M.D., Basic Books (1992, 1997).

Toxic Parents, Overcoming Their Hurtful Legacy and Reclaiming Your Life by Dr. Susan Forward and Craig Buck, Bantam Books (1989).

About the Author

Author Karen A. Stansbury practiced law in Connecticut for twenty-four years. After enduring twenty years of courtroom litigation she became certified in mediation, hoping for a more peaceful life. She began posting helpful articles on her website, encouraging clients to choose a less stressful path to problem solving. Writing novels using real cases was the next logical step. Now she does it full time.

When Karen isn't writing or traveling, she's painting watercolor landscapes, or riding, or kayaking, or biking, or rowing, or cooking, or gardening. She lives in Litchfield County, Connecticut.